7

Decision-Making in
Forest Management

FORESTRY RESEARCH STUDIES SERIES

Sponsored by The Royal Forestry Society of England, Wales and Northern Ireland

1. Decision-Making in Forest Management
   M.R.W. Williams

Decision-Making in Forest Management

M.R.W. Williams, M.A.

Cumbria College of Agriculture and Forestry, England

RESEARCH STUDIES PRESS
A DIVISION OF JOHN WILEY & SONS LTD
Chichester · New York · Brisbane · Toronto

RESEARCH STUDIES PRESS

Editorial Office:
8 Willian Way, Letchworth, Herts. SG6 2HG, England

British Library Cataloguing in Publication Data:

Williams, M. R. W.
  Decision-making in forest management.
  —(Forestry research studies series; 1)
  1. Forestry management—Decision making—Great
  Britain
  I. Title   II. Series
  333.75′0941   SD414.G7

ISBN 0 471 10097 8

Printed in the United States of America

This book is dedicated to the memory of my
father, Charles Robert Farmer Williams,
formerly Conservator of Forests in the
Imperial Forest Service, Principal of the
Madras Forest College at Coimbatore and later
lecturer in Forest Economics at Stellenbosch
University. He died in South Africa on 17th
February 1981. His help, guidance and
encouragement were a constant source of
inspiration to me.

MICHAEL ROBERT WALE WILLIAMS, born 20th April,
1923 at Coonoor in South India. Father then
Principal of the Madras Forest College,
Coimbatore and later Conservator of Forests
for the Nilghiri Circle. Educated at Bembridge
School, Isle of Wight, and Keble College,
Oxford, with five years of service with the
R.A.F. sandwiched in between. Served as a
District Forest Officer with the Forestry
Commission (1950 - 66), General Manager of a
Forestry Co-operative Society and as a Consul-
tant in private practice. Appointed as Lecturer
in Forestry at the Cumbria College of Agriculture
and Forestry (1975).

It gives me great pleasure, for two particular reasons, to write this Foreword: I have a high regard for 'our' Royal Forestry Society of England, Wales & Northern Ireland who are promoting this book; and through teaching and practice in forestry I am aware of the great need for a textbook of this nature.

For several years the essence of the book has benefited students at the Cumbria College of Agriculture and Forestry at Newton Rigg. Now, happily, this knowledge and information will be available both to students elsewhere and to practising foresters, woodland owners, managers and consultants throughout the United Kingdom.

It was a wise decision of The Royal Forestry Society to appoint a small "Editorial Panel" comprising Esmond Harris, Director, William Seymour, a Past President, and Scott Leathart, Editor, to plan a series of forestry books to fulfil the first of the Society's objectives which is: "The advancement of the knowledge and practice of Forestry and Arboriculture in all their branches and the dissemination of such knowledge...". The panel has prudently entrusted each book of the series, of which this is the first, to be written by a specialist.

In forestry there is a significant lapse of time

between the start of costs being incurred and the end of the period in which all costs and benefits arise. With the cyclical changes in levels of returns and the general rise in costs, it is never easy to appraise investment in order to show the relative profitability of alternative courses of action. This book will help greatly, particularly in the basic concepts of investment appraisal, not simply to discover the course of decision-making likely to yield the highest profit but also to determine the cost if departing from it in order to satisfy some other objective. The book will be of immense interest to all concerned with forestry and not least to any conservationist who questions the work of the forester and clamours for actions contrary to maximum profitability. It should enable him or her to calculate the opportunity cost relevant to his or her own proposals and then to couple the result with an awareness that someone has to foot the bill.

The publication of this welcome book will bring deserving notice to Michael Williams' work in his particular sphere of forestry. At the same time it will attract appropriate prestige to his College at Newton Rigg, as well as to The Royal Forestry Society itself. Perhaps even more important, the management of woodlands throughout Great Britain will surely benefit, while the task of the forestry student, the forester and the land agent will be eased. At the very least, decision-making will be correctly oriented.

Chenies,   Dr. Cyril Hart, MA, MSc
Coleford,   (Oxon), FRICS, FIFor.
Gloucestershire.   Senior Verderer of the
                                  Royal Forest of Dean
June,1981.

(IX) ACKNOWLEDGMENTS

Much of the material in this book originates from many sources, collected over thirty years of close involvement in forest management, both practically and academically. It is presented here, after much thought and discussion with colleagues and students, in a form that is hoped to be simple and explicit. An attempt has been made to strip away some of the accumulated layers of jargon which hide the meaning. It is a salutary fact that in trying to teach a subject, one learns a lot more about it, so I am much indebted to my students for their reactions and "feed-back".

Particular acknowledgment must be given for the use of basic data from the Forestry Commission's "Forest Management Tables" and from Dr. Cyril Hart's "Forestry Costings and Timber Prices". Raw material has been obtained from both these publications which has proved invaluable. The thoughts, ideas and inspirations from "classical" German foresters, from W. E. Hiley and the more recent Messrs. Johnston, Grayson and Bradley, have all contributed basic concepts, modified and applied in the book.

The help and encouragement given by the Royal Forestry Society of England, Wales and Northern Ireland, in sponsoring this publication, is much appreciated. So also is the tolerance, forbearing and active assistance of my colleagues at the Cumbria College of Agriculture and Forestry. All this has made it a hard, but enjoyable, task.

Michael R. W. Williams.

Penrith, Cumbria.
November 1980.

(XI) CONTENTS

(XII)   CONTENTS

(XIII) CONTENTS

(XV) <u>TABLES, GRAPHS AND DIAGRAMS</u>

(XVI)   <u>TABLES, GRAPHS AND DIAGRAMS</u>

(XVII)   TABLES, GRAPHS AND DIAGRAMS

(XVIII) <u>TABLES, GRAPHS AND DIAGRAMS</u>

Chapter 1

1.1 The importance of decision-making in forest management.

There are two main characteristics of all managers.
Firstly, they act for someone else to whom they are
responsible for their actions. Secondly, they have
to make decisions and be able to justify them. The
latter is perhaps of even greater importance in forestry than in most other enterprises, because of the
time-scale involved.

Farmers, for instance, can usually tell by the end
of a season whether they made the right choice of
crop. In industry, it is usually apparent whether a
decision was right within a year or two. In forestry,
however, a wrong decision at the beginning of a rotation often cannot be put right - indeed may not even
be recognised - for many years. The time-scale can
be fifty, a hundred or even a hundred and fifty years.
So, the right decision is even more important in forestry than in most other forms of enterprise.

1.2 Types of decision in forest management.

The sort of decision a forest manager has to make,
with long lasting consequences, include:-

(a) How much can I afford to pay for the land for planting?

(b) What species of tree should I grow?

(c) Am I justified in spending extra money on cultivation, ground-preparation or applying fertilisers?

(d) Should I thin the crop normally? to waste? or go for a non-thinning regime with clear-felling on a short rotation for pulpwood?

(e) Am I wasting money on brashing and high-pruning?

(f) When should I replace an unsatisfactory or uneconomic crop?

(g) What is the optimum length of rotation for a certain species on a particular site to achieve the "objects of management"?

(h) What is the most economic density of roading for a particular forest?

1.3 Making the decisions.

Some people are born with a certain flair for business and appear to be able to make the right decision by instinct. Many of the most successful entrepreneurs can do this, but they are few and far between. Most people need some sort of help and guidance in coming to the right decision, if only as an objective backing to give them greater confidence.

Since a manager is someone who is responsible to another person for his actions, he has to be able to justify them. If all goes well, his decisions are not likely to be challenged; but if something goes wrong and he fails to achieve the objectives, a very good explanation is needed. If he can show that his decision was the right one in the circumstances then prevailing, the manager is in a much stronger position. "I did it because I thought it was right, but I was wrong" may be a very honest statement but it is not likely to placate an irate owner!

1.4 Financial aids to decision-making.

In making decisions it is helpful to have a criterion or "yardstick" against which to measure alternative courses of action. Such a criterion, which is understood by everyone, is that of - money. A case can be made more easily if it can be said that following a certain course of action, a profit will be made.

The financial "tools", described in this book may be used by forest managers to help them arrive at the right conclusions. The first few chapters cover the background to such decision-making, then follows a description of how the "tools" are "assembled" and finally, how these aids can be used to answer some of the questions set-out above.

1.5 A warning to the users of these financial aids.

It should be emphasised from the start that using such financial "tools" is no substitute for decision-making by the manager. These decisions have to be made by him, and he stands or falls by them. It is truly said that a "bad workman blames his tools". These aids are there to help him, but the decisions are his alone. The "tools" are only as good as the information on which they are based - suspect information will provide suspect decisions. Extreme care has to be used in ensuring that only the best and most accurate information is used. In the long run, it is human judgement that counts.

Chapter 2

2.1 Future benefits and debts.

When payments and receipts occur at the same time,
or at least in the same year, it is not difficult to
compare them and to discover if a profit or a loss
has been made. However, when they are separated by
a number of years, as is usually the case in forestry,
a wrong impression may easily be given.

Table 2.1 shows three projects where expenditure is
the same, but receipts differ. At a glance, it is
obvious that Project C appears to be the most profitable. If expenditure and receipts occurred at the
same time, this would be true. However, if the in-
terval was longer and varied between the projects,
the conclusions could be quite different.

If Project A took 15 years, Project B 25 years and
Project C 50 years, which would then be the most profitable? To answer this, it is necessary to make
some allowance for the passage of time. In the first
case the investor would have to wait 15 years before
be got a return, in the second, 25 years and in the
third, 50 years. His money would be tied up all this
time, when it could perhaps have been earning more in
another investment.

Table 2.1

	PROJECTS		
	A	B	C
Expenditure	£100	100	100
Receipts	£400	500	1000
Profit	£300	400	900
"Ranking"	3	2	1

Table 2.2

	PROJECTS		
	A	B	C
Profit	£300	400	900
Number of Years	15	25	50
Average profit per year	£20	16	18
"Ranking"	1	3	2

Table 2.3

Year	Debt	Interest due	Calculation of Increased debt	Compound Interest factor $(1.0p^n)$	Compound discount factor $(1/1.0p^n)$
0	100	10	£100 × 1	1.0	1.0
1	110	11	× 1.1	1.1	0.909
2	121	12	× 1.1^2	1.21	0.826
3	133	13	× 1.1^3	1.33	0.752
4	146	15	× 1.1^4	1.46	0.685
5	161	16	× 1.1^5	1.61	0.621
6	177	18	× 1.1^6	1.77	0.565
7	195	19	× 1.1^7	1.95	0.513
8	214	21	× 1.1^8	2.14	0.467
9	235	24	× 1.1^9	2.35	0.426
10	261	26	× 1.1^{10}	2.61	0.383

A simple, perhaps crude, way of doing this would be to divide the profit by the number of years taken to achieve it. This would give the average annual profit over the period. This is shown in Table 2.2. Now Project A appears the most profitable since it is divided by the smallest number of years.

While this Average Annual Profit method does take into account the different lengths of time involved in the three projects, it is a crude method because in fact accumulated debts and credits grow at compound interest rates as will be shown later.

2.2 Present value of future benefits and debts.

Perhaps the effect of time on financial calculations can best be summed up by saying that money owing, or owed, has not the same value now as it will have when paid in the future. This is nothing to do with inflation or the actual value of currency, but expresses the fact that you cannot easily spend money you have not got.

In other words, if you have an I.O.U. for £5 (payable sometime in the future) you cannot easily spend it in a shop to buy goods now. If you are known to the shopkeeper and he is satisfied that he will get the money - sometime - he may be prepared to take a risk and accept it at a lower value, say £4. The amount he would allow on it would depend on how long he had to wait for his money.

In the same way, a debt owed by you to be paid in five years time is not so great a burden to you now. You have five years in which to save up for it or you can put a smaller sum on deposit in a bank to attract interest and build up to the sum needed by the time it is to be paid.

So both future benefits and future debts have a lesser value now than they will have in the future. The saying "A bird in the hand is worth two in the bush" illustrates this very point.

If it is accepted that future debts and benefits are not worth as much now as they will be later on, this must be allowed for in financial calculations. How is this to be done? One suggestion has already been made, that a future debt could be met by placing a smaller sum on deposit and allowing it to build up to the required amount in time to pay it off. The relationship between the original sum and the final figure will depend on the number of years between them and the rate of interest paid by the bank. Once established, this relationship can be used to relate the present value of all future benefits and debts. This is the principle of "discounting", discussed later.

2.3 Capital and interest: simple and compound interest.

When money is borrowed, or lent, the sum actually transferred is referred to as the CAPITAL. The "hire -charge" for borrowing the money is referred to as INTEREST. The interest charged on a loan is usually expressed as an annual percentage on the capital sum. For example, if £100 is borrowed and the annual inter-est payment is £10, this is expressed as 10% per annum.

If the interest payment is paid each year, the original debt remains the same until repayment is due. This is known as SIMPLE interest. However, if the interest were not paid each year but added to the sum borrowed, the debt would increase considerably over the period. Each year the amount of interest due would be on an increasing loan and this in turn would be added to the debt. In this case the debt would be said to be increasing at COMPOUND interest.

At a rate of 10%, the original loan of £100 would become £110 at the end of the first year, £121 at the end of the second year, £133 at the end of the third year and £261 at the end of ten years. This means that the debt would double in just over seven years and double again in another seven years and so on. Table 2.3 shows how a debt increases at compound interest.

The increased debt at the end of any number of
years may be calculated by multiplying the original
sum by the "compound interest factor". This factor
can be obtained by using the formula $1.0p^n$, where 'p'
is the rate of interest and 'n' is the number of
years. It should be noted that the figure '0' is
only used for rates under 10%, e.g. 3% would be 1.03
while 12% would be 1.12. So the compound interest
factor for 7 years @ 10% would be 1.10 multiplied by
itself 7 times (1.10^7) which is 1.95.

2.4 Compounding and Discounting.

So far, what has been described is the process of
"compounding", which is the _future_ value of a debt or
benefit. This depends on the rate of interest used
and the number of years involved. The reverse process,
that of finding the _present_ value of future debts or
benefits, is known as DISCOUNTING.

Just as a present debt of £100 would increase at 10%
compound interest to £261 in ten years time, it is
equally true to say that a debt of £261 due to be paid
in ten years time is only worth £100 today. This is
because that is the sum that could be placed on deposit now to build up to the required amount in ten years
time.

The "Discount factor", which is the reciprocal of the
compound interest factor, can be used to multiply the
future sum to find its present value. This factor can
be obtained from the formula $1/1.0p^n$. So the discount
factor for 10 years @ 10% would be $1/1.10^{10}$ or 1/2.61
= 0.383. Using this factor, we can see that £261 in
ten years time is now worth £100 (£261 x 0.383 or
£261/2.61).

In Table 2.3, the last column gives the discount
factors which may be compared with the compound interest factors in the previous column. While today it is
relatively easy to calculate these factors by using a
simple electronic calculator, tables of compound

Table 2.4

N.B. These figures are given
by the "Rule of thumb" formula
$\dfrac{72}{p}$

Rate of Compound interest	Approximate number of years to double original debt
2	35
4	18
6	12
8	9
10	7
12	6
14	5

Table 2.5a

Project	Receipts	Years	@ 10% Discount factor	Discounted Revenue	Expenditure	Profit/Loss	Ranking
A	£400	15	0.23917	£96	£100	− £4	1
B	£500	25	0.09216	£46	£100	− £54	2
C	£1000	50	0.00849	£8.50	£100	− £91.50	3

Table 2.5b

Project	Receipts	Years	@ 6% Discount factor	Discounted Revenue	Expenditure	Profit/Loss	Ranking
A	£400	15	0.4170	£166	£100	+ 66	1
B	£500	25	0.2328	£155	£100	+ £55	2
C	£1000	50	0.0542	£ 54	£100	− £46	3

interest and discount factors are available in many
publications for easy use.

These processes of compounding and discounting can
be used to bring all costs and receipts, whether past
or future, to the same point in time for direct comparison. If Projects A, B and C, mentioned in Section
2.1, are now compared using the process of discounting,
a different pattern appears. This is shown in Table
2.5.

2.5 The effects of varying time-scales on financial
     calculations.

The three projects already considered were relatively straight forward in that all expenditure was at
the beginning and receipts at the end of the period.
Even so, the length of time taken to achieve the
results had a considerable bearing on the profitability of the project.

Generally speaking in forestry, the pattern is the
same, that is, the bulk of the expenditure is at the
beginning of the rotation and receipts at the end.
However, it is often not as simple as that as there
may well be intermediate expenditure and receipts.

As well as the initial establishment costs such as
ploughing, draining, fencing and planting there can
be subsequent expenditure. This would include beating-up, weeding, brashing, pruning, applying fertilisers and, even later, road-making. In addition there
would be general maintenance charges such as fence
repairs, cleaning drains and protection.

Similarly, as well as the returns from the final
felling of the crop, there would be intermediate
income from the sale of thinnings and even from the
sale of Christmas trees. Very early returns can in
fact have a considerable effect on the profitability
of a crop.

Table 2.6 shows an example of costs and receipts at
various stages in the life of a tree-crop. By the

Table 2.6

Year		COSTS		RECEIPTS		
	Operation	Actual Cost	Discounted Cost	Produce	Sale Price	Discounted Receipts
0	Preparation of ground & planting	200	200			
1	Beating-up, Weeding	100	95			
2	Weeding	50	45			
3	Weeding	50	43			
5				Christmas Trees	750	588
10	Brashing & Racking	100	61			
12	Road-making	2,000	1114			
15				Thinning	150	72
20	Pruning	50	19	Thinning	250	94
25				Thinning	250	74
30				Thinning	810	187
35				Thinning	1,000	181
40				Thinning	1,000	142
45				Thinning	1,200	134
50				Clearfelling	7,500	654
TOTAL DISCOUNTED COSTS			1577	TOTAL: DISCOUNTED RECEIPTS		2126
				LESS COSTS		1577
				NET RECEIPTS		549

process of discounting, all costs and receipts, when-
ever they occur, can be made directly comparable by
bringing them all back to the beginning of the rotation. In other words, the equivalent values at the
beginning of the rotation can be given for all later
costs and receipts.

The importance of early financial returns in determining profitability is shown by the fact that @ 5%
c.i. the £750 from the sale of Christmas trees in year
5 is worth £588 while the £7,500 from the sale of the
final felling at year 50 is only worth £654. Without
the sale of Christmas trees, the project would have
lost £9.

2.6 Discounting and monetary inflation.

It must be emphasised that the technique of discounting is only used to take into account the passage
of time. In other words, it takes into account the
length of time between the present and the time when
the money is received or paid.

Consequently, it is assumed that the real value of
the money is the same at the end of the period as it
is now. In these days of high currency inflation,
this is not always so. However, if it is thought of
as being in "real" terms, the relative value will be
the same.

If both costs and receipts rise at the same rate,
the difference between them will remain the same and
inflation can be virtually ignored.

At the same time other factors will have an effect.
If productivity can be increased by more efficient
working, say by mechanisation, then relative costs are
likely to fall. If the supply of timber becomes more
scarce, prices are likely to rise. In these circumstances, the difference between costs and prices could
widen and the value of the product in real terms could
in fact be higher.

These factors will be taken into account in the next

chapter where the effects of different rates of compound interest are discussed and arguments are put forward for the choice of a particular rate of interest.

<u>Chapter 3</u>

3.1   <u>The effect of various rates on profitability.</u>

In <u>Table 2.5</u>, it was seen that at a discount rate of
10% all three projects made a loss. This was because
at this rate, the present value of £400 in 15 years
time is only £96, £500 in 25 years is £46 and £1,000
in 50 years is £8.50. If these are all compared with
the expenditure of £100, the net loss is £4, £54 and
£91.50. What would the position be at other rates of
discount? <u>Table 3.1</u> shows the results of discounting
these sums at various rates from 2% to 10%.

From this table it can be seen that while all three
projects made a loss at 10%, Project **A** made a profit
at 9%, Project B at 6% and Project C at 4%.

By taking this further and plotting the net results
against the various discount rates on a graph such as
<u>Figure 3.2</u>, the discount rate at which the "break-even"
point occurs can be found. This is the point where
the net result is "nil" or where the values of expenditure and receipts are equal.

From this graph it is possible to compare the profitability of the three projects directly. Project **A**
breaks even at 9.6%, Project B at 6.7% and Project C

Table 3.1

Project	Discount Rate	2%	3%	4%	5%	6%	7%	8%	9%	10%
	Discount factor /15 yrs)	.743	.642	.555	.481	.417	.362	.315	.275	.239
	Receipts: £400 × factor	296	256	221	192	167	144	126	109	96
A	Less: Expenditure	100	100	100	100	100	100	100	100	100
	Profit (+) Loss (−)	+ 196	+ 156	+ 121	+ 92	+ 67	+ 44	+ 26	+ 9	− 4
	"Ranking"	3	1	1	1	1	1	1	1	1
	Discount factor (25 yrs)	.610	.478	.375	.295	.233	.184	.146	.116	.092
	Receipts: £500 × factor	304	238	187	148	116	92	73	58	46
B	Less: Expenditure	100	100	100	100	100	100	100	100	100
	Profit (+) Loss (−)	+ 204	+ 138	+ 87	+ 48	+ 16	− 8	− 27	− 42	− 54
	"Ranking"	2	2	2	2	2	2	2	2	2
	Discount factor (50 yrs)	.372	.228	.141	.087	.054	.033	.021	.013	.009
	Receipts: £1000 × factor	370	227	140	87	54	34	21	13	9
C	Less: Expenditure	100	100	100	100	100	100	100	100	100
	Profit (+) Loss (−)	+ 270	+ 127	+ 40	− 13	− 46	− 66	− 79	− 87	− 91
	"Ranking"	1	3	3	3	3	3	3	3	3

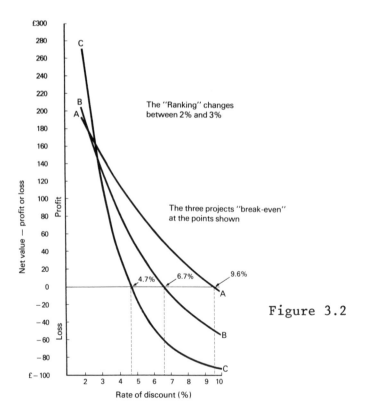

The "Ranking" changes between 2% and 3%

The three projects "break-even" at the points shown

Figure 3.2

at 4.8%. It can be seen that, in fact, Project A is twice as profitable as Project C.

From this it can be seen that the profitability of an investment will depend very much on the rate of compound discount used. The rate used in such calculations is often arbitrarily chosen, for various reasons as discussed later, but at the same time it is possible to determine the actual rate-of-return of the project itself. When money has to be borrowed for such an investment, if it can be borrowed at a rate lower than this "rate-of-return", it will result in a profit. If it has to be borrowed at a higher rate, it will result in a loss.

3.2 The comparative effects of interest rate and time.

Both the length of time between payment and receipts and the rate of compound interest charged affect the profitability of a project. In the first example given in Section 2.1, the effect of time without any interest charge is shown by comparing Tables 2.1 and 2.2. Similarly, in Section 3.1, the effects of different rates of interest over the same length of time are shown (Table 3.1).

Generally speaking, it can be seen that the longer the period of time and the higher the rate of interest used, the less profitable the investment is likely to be. Conversely, the shorter the period and the lower the interest charge, the more profitable it is likely to be. The conclusion can also be drawn that the higher the rate of interest charge, the shorter the period must be to make it profitable. Equally, if the interest charge is low, the project can stand a much longer period of time and still be profitable.

To see which has the greater effect, time or rate of interest, Table 3.1 shows the comparative effects of each. This shows quite clearly that 10 years at 1% is higher than 1 year at 10%.

This can be explained by reference to the formula,

given in Section 2.3, which is used to determine the compound interest factor, $1.0p^n$. In this formula 'p' is the rate of interest and 'n' the number of years, so it can be seen that the rate of interest is raised to the power of the number of years. In other words, the number of years raises the factor exponentially and the higher the rate the greater the effect of the number of years.

In forestry, where the time-scale is considerably longer than in other forms of investment, it can be seen that the rate of interest used can make all the difference between profit and loss. In the rest of this chapter, various factors influencing the choice of interest rates are discussed.

3.3 The effects of supply and demand on interest rates.

Money, in one sense, is a commodity like any other. Just as when there is a strong demand for scarce goods, prices rise; so when there is a great demand to borrow money, interest rates rise. If no one wants, or can afford, to borrow money, rates will fall. The economic "law" of Supply and Demand applies equally to money itself.

In fact, one of the causes of inflation is said to be "too much money chasing too few goods and services". If wages and earnings rise more quickly than the supply of consumer goods, prices rise to compensate for it.

A similar situation arises with currency exchange rates. When there is a great demand for a particular currency, its value in comparison with other currencies will rise. When everyone wants to sell a particular currency, its value falls.

So one of the factors determining interest rates is the scarcity or plentiful supply of capital. Scarce capital will attract higher rates of interest, while a plentiful supply will depress rates of interest.

These factors only apply in a "free market". Where exchange rates are fixed arbitrarily, no change in demand will affect the rate. Government fiscal policy, too, can affect the situation. Where the bank Minimum Lending Rate is fixed by government action, to encourage or discourage lending, this can distort the natural reaction to supply and demand.

Going on this premise alone, one could imagine that if everyone wanted to invest money in forestry, rates would rise. If no one wanted to, and the capital were available, rates would fall.

However, many other factors come into the situation as will be seen in the rest of this chapter.

3.4 The degree of risk in an investment.

Just as the amount of money to be paid for an insurance premium depends on the risk to be covered, so the interest payable on loan capital will depend on the security of the investment.

Traditionally, government bonds, debenture shares and other "blue chip" investments have carried a low rate of interest because of their security. Risky enterprises and speculative ventures carry much higher rates of interest because there is a much greater chance of losing the money altogether. There is obviously a chance of making a lot of money out of such an investment but an equal chance of making nothing at all.

Forestry is a relatively safe investment. There is a reasonable chance that timber in some form or another will always be needed. If the rules of good silviculture are followed, trees will go on growing whatever the political or monetary situation. Natural disasters can occur to destroy woodlands, such as fire, wind and flood, but usually something can be salvaged and the land will still be there.

It can thus be argued that a properly managed forest, on a reasonable site with good expectations,

is a very safe investment. In fact, as has already
been mentioned, it is almost inflation-proof. In these
circumstances, there has always been an acceptance of
low rates of interest in forestry because of its security. In fact, in some continental countries in
Europe, a rate of 1 to 2% on long-term crops such as
oak have been considered quite acceptable.

3.5 Long-term and short-term investments

Generally speaking, it is more expensive to borrow
money on short-term loans than on longer-term ones.
This appears surprising, as one would think that with
a quicker turn-over the lender would be in a more
"liquid" position. In other words, he would get his
cash back more quickly and would be able to lend it
out again or spend it himself.

Superficially, of course, such short-term loans may
not appear to be more expensive but if they are converted into annual terms, it can be seen that they are.
An overnight loan @ 0.1% seems very low, but in annual
terms this could represent 36.5%. Similarly, a loan
for three months @ 5% is equivalent to an annual rate
of 20%.

Equally, one could argue that the total yield from a
long-term investment, at compound interest, even at a
low rate of interest, is greater than from a shorter
period at a higher rate. This was shown in Section
3.2 where 10 years @ 1% came to a higher figure than
1 year @ 10%. In other words, the number of years has
a greater effect than the rate of interest. The
longer the term of the loan, the lower the rate of
interest needed to provide an equivalent return.

Forestry is usually a very long-term investment - 50,
100 or even 150 years. Consequently there is a strong
argument in favour of a low rate of interest. The
largely inflation-proof nature of the investment, its
long-term nature and high security all favour a low
rate of interest.

Another factor to be considered is that high rates

of interest put a premium on the immediate future and discourage long-term investments. If forests and woodlands are thought of as a self-perpetuating natural resource - which with proper management they can be - it is essential that an adequate growing-stock is built up and maintained. High rates of interest mitigate against this and encourage short rotations with possible loss of soil fertility and site degradation.

3.6 Alternative rates of interest.

An investor, wishing to maximise the return on his capital, will obviously consider all the possible alternatives. Before he puts his money into forestry he would see what returns he could get from other forms of investment.

In comparing the returns from various forms of investment all the factors already discussed would have to be taken into consideration, as well as the actual financial rate. On the face of it forestry comes well down on a list of possible investments. In Britain today comparative returns show a wide range. Bank deposit accounts at present pay 17%, government loans 5%, building societies 12% (tax paid), while stocks and shares could pay 20%. Against all this, forestry probably would not yield more than 5 or 6%.

So, obviously, an investor "in for a quick kill" would not put his money in forestry. He could invest in a highly speculative project when he would either make a lot of money quickly or possibly lose the lot. On the other hand, if it were not so important to him to get a quick return but have a really secure, inflation-proof investment over a long period, then forestry could have its attraction. This is the attitude of Trustees or Pension Funds, who are looking for long-term security.

For the individual who buys woodlands, often many non financial considerations are of greater importance. These could include amenity, pleasant surroundings, opportunities for sporting interests and even status or presteige. In such circumstances the actual

financial return could be far outweighed by these
other considerations.

3.7 Choosing an appropriate rate of interest.

From the figures shown in Table 3.1, it can be seen
that the choice of an appropriate test discount rate
can make all the difference between a project making a
profit or a loss. Where the relative performance of
two courses of action are being considered, this is of
lesser importance since the "ranking" will remain the
same.

Where funds are only available at a fixed rate of
interest, then obviously this rate would have to be
used to be realistic. This was the line taken by H.M.
Treasury in their "Cost/Benefit Analysis" (1974) when
a test rate of 10% was used. Not surprisingly they
found that, at this rate, nowhere in Britain was forestry profitable. They apparently failed to realise
that, at this rate, forestry was equally unprofitable
in most timber producing countries in the world. They
found that in certain parts of Northern England and
Southern Scotland a return of 6% could be realised,
and elsewhere something like 3 to 4%.

A more appropriate test rate would be one near the
actual rate generated by the project itself. On this
basis, the Forestry Commission uses a test rate of 5%,
which includes an element to allow for inflation. In
"real terms" they consider the rate of return about
$3\frac{1}{2}\%$.

Consequently, for the calculations in this book a
rate of 5% has been used.

Chapter 4

4.1 The relationship between price and size

Generally speaking, there is a direct relationship
between the average size of tree sold and the price
paid per cubic metre. One would naturally expect to
find that the larger the tree, the higher the price
paid per unit volume. However, this relationship is
seldom as simple as that, for many other factors come
into it.

The price paid for any commodity depends on the
availability of supplies and the demand for them.
Where supplies outstrip demand, prices will fall; but
where demand is greater than the available supplies,
because of the increased competition, prices will rise.
This applies just as much to timber as to any other
commodity.

Timber prices can also vary according to the demand
for a particular size of tree. In certain areas and
at certain times there may be a greater demand for
small-sized trees. At other times and in other places,
small-sized trees may be completely unsaleable as there
is only a demand for those sizes capable of yielding
sawlogs. This variation in demand for different sizes
can distort the relationship between the price and size

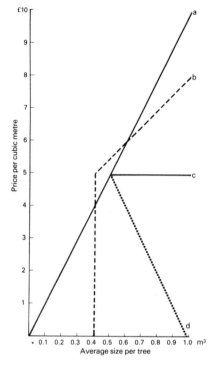

Figure 4.1

a. Steady increase in price with size
b. Unsaleable below 0.4m³ — steady increase thereafter
c. No increase in price over 0.5m³
d. Steady fall in price over 0.5m³

Table 4.2

(a) 1 October 1977 to 30 September 1978   (b) 1 October 1978 to 30 September 1979

Average Volume per Tree in Cubic Metres	ENGLAND			SCOTLAND			WALES			GREAT BRITAIN		
	Volume m³	Total price £	Average price £/m³	Volume m³	Total price £	Average price £/m³	Volume m³	Total price £	Average price £/m³	Volume m³	Total price £	Average price £/m³
Up to 0.074 a.	45010	181363	4.029	26946	69698	2.587	5345	21050	3.938	77301	272111	3.520
b.	62805	258178	4.111	25212	58054	2.303	20108	52067	2.589	108125	368299	3.406
Over 0.074 a.	51001	272692	5.347	69405	249568	3.596	46765	208254	4.453	167171	730514	4.370
to 0.124 b.	47296	237495	5.021	81254	227903	2.805	80435	249188	3.098	208985	714586	3.419
Over 0.124 a.	16908	109628	6.484	43524	199659	4.587	26023	148803	5.718	86455	458090	5.299
to 0.174 b.	20982	147578	7.034	40515	207044	5.110	25132	126855	5.048	86629	481477	5.558
Over 0.174 a.	13416	92338	6.883	26700	183645	6.878	13284	85131	6.409	53400	361114	6.762
to 0.224 b.	11365	101769	8.955	46200	272001	5.887	15633	118138	7.557	73198	491908	6.720
Over 0.224 a.	11490	111312	9.688	4546	30672	6.747	7264	58528	8.057	23300	200512	8.606
to 0.274 b.	15723	151255	9.620	5494	51555	9.384	2011	15139	7.528	23228	217949	9.383
Over 0.274 a.	11123	111141	9.992	34814	260207	7.474	11734	96681	8.239	57671	468029	8.115
to 0.424 b.	24136	296124	12.269	31564	289139	9.160	20504	197631	9.369	76204	782894	10.274
Over 0.424 a.	29547	405460	13.722	46687	465386	9.968	12964	136599	15.537	89198	1007445	11.294
b.	30769	444002	14.430	74906	880773	11.758	26967	366085	13.575	132642	1690860	12.747
Total a.	178495	1283934	7.193	252622	1458835	5.775	123379	755046	6.120	554496	3497815	6.308
b.	213076	1636401	7.680	305145	1986469	6.510	190790	1125103	5.897	709011	4747973	6.697

of tree. It is also possible to find a situation where a tree is too large for sawmills in the area and the price for those larger sizes may actually fall.

Where there is a flourishing agricultural and horticultural industry, there may well be a large demand for small-sized poles for fencing posts, rustic poles and even pea and bean sticks. There may also be a temporary demand in certain places where, for example, a large quantity of fencing material is needed for new motorways, pipelines and power lines. Elsewhere, remote from such areas, it may be impossible to sell anything under sawlog size.

Figure 4.1 shows examples of such variations related to price.

4.2   Timber prices in Britain.

As well as local and year-to-year variations in demand for different sizes of timber, prices in Britain are very much influenced by world prices. About 92% of the wood used in Britain, for all purposes, is imported. Consequently, prices paid for home-grown timber are very much affected by those paid for imported wood. No one is going to pay more for home-grown material than they have to pay for imported timber. When world prices rise, then home-grown prices rise in step. A slump in world prices will equally produce a drop in the home market.

World prices vary from year to year and depend largely on the amount of supplies available in the exporting countries. As they use more and more of their own timber, the amount available for export falls. As supplies become less available, so prices rise.

Historically, there has been a steady upward trend in world timber prices since the turn of the last century. This can partly be accounted for by inflation, but the level has increased in real terms. This trend is likely to continue and even accelerate as more and more natural forest becomes worked out and more

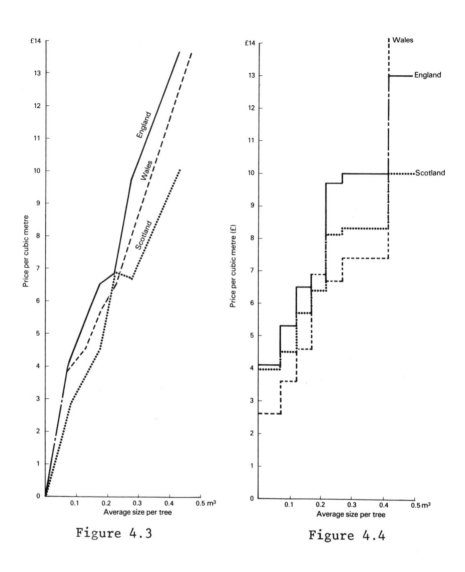

Figure 4.3   Figure 4.4

reliance has to be placed on plantations. Obviously the cost of exploiting natural forest is far less than that of artificially established plantations, where planting and maintenance costs are involved.

Many traditional timber-exporting countries are now reaching this stage and in fact the Food and Agriculture Organisation of the United Nations has for some time been forecasting a timber famine in the 21st Century. This will obviously affect world prices for timber, which could well reflect the trend in oil prices in the 1970s. A rise in world prices would obviously affect the prices paid for British-grown timber.

4.3 Forestry Commission prices for sales of standing coniferous trees.

In Britain, the Forestry Commission publishes the prices they receive for the sale of standing coniferous trees. These figures are given for various size-categories, separately for England, Wales and Scotland and also the average for Great Britain. Table 4.2 sets out the prices received for the periods (a) 1st October 1977 to 30th September 1978 and (b) 1st October 1978 to 30th September 1979. This table gives an indication of regional variations and also the differences between the two years recorded.

Using the figures from Table 4.2, Figure 4.3 shows this as a Price/Size Gradient. By joining-up the fixed points with a series of straight lines, it shows graphically the relationship between the average size of tree and the price paid per cubic metre. It gives an indication of the general trend, but of course the intermediate points are not strictly accurate.

Both the Table and the Graph show some of the variations discussed in Section 4.1. It can be seen that, on the whole, prices in England were higher than in Scotland or Wales. In the second year (78/79), prices in Scotland were higher than in Wales which is the reverse of the case in the previous year. This shows the regional variations over the period. Similarly,

prices for the different size-categories varied over
the two years. On the whole, prices for the smaller
sizes of tree fell in the second year, while they rose
noticeably for the larger sizes. These figures reflect
the variations in supply and demand for the different
sizes during the two years. If the different size-categories in the three regions are directly compared,
greater variations appear. However, the overall trend
for Great Britain over the two years showed a slight
increase.

4.4   The Price/Size Gradient.

Figure 4.3 shows the relationship between the average size of tree and the price per cubic metre as a
continuous curve made up of straight lines. In Section 4.3 it is pointed out that the intermediate points
are not strictly accurate as, in fact, they are "cut-
off" points. A better form of presentation would be
as a "stepped" graph as shown in Figure 4.4. Since
there is no difference in price between, say, $0.074m^3$
and $0.124m^3$, these points would be better joined by a
horizontal line. The same applies between $0.124m^3$ and
$0.174m^3$ and so on to form a series of "steps". This
gives a more realistic relationship between average
size of tree and the price.

An even more realistic representation can be given
by grouping these "size" categories into "produce"
categories. The three main types of produce from coniferous trees in Britain are:-

1.   Pulpwood (7-14cm top diameter)

2.   Pallet wood (14-24cm top diameter) and

3.   Sawlogs (over 24cm top diameter)

These three categories can be related to the average
size of tree by using the Assortment Tables in the
Forestry Commission's "Forest Management Tables". From
these tables it is found that all material under 0.224
m^3 per tree falls into the "Pulpwood" category. Material between $0.224m^3$ and $0.424m^3$ per tree is "Pallet
wood" and all over $0.424m^3$ per tree is in the "Sawlog"

category.

It is now possible to re-draw the stepped graph using the produce categories as shown in Figure 4.5.

To get the average price paid in each category, it is necessary to get the total volume (m^3) and divide it into the price paid $(£)$. For example, the figures for England taken from Table 4.2 are grouped as follows:-

(1) Pulpwood		(2) Pallet wood		(3) Sawlogs
45010	181363	11490	111312	
51001	272692	11123	111141	$29547m^3$
16908	109628			£405460
13416	92338	$22613m^3$	£222453	£405460 ÷
$126325m^3$	£656021	£222453 ÷ $22613m^3$		$29547m^3$
£656021÷$126325m^3$=£5.19		= £9.80		= £13.72

The figures for the three regions and the average for Great Britain used for the graph in Figure 4.5 are as follows:-

Category	England	Scotland	Wales	Great Britain
Pulpwood	£ 5.19	£ 4.22	£ 5.07	£ 4.74
Pallet wood	9.80	7.39	8.17	8.26
Sawlogs	13.72	9.97	15.54	11.29

4.5 Using the Price/Size graph to value a stand of coniferous timber.

If a stand, or parcel of standing coniferous trees, can be broken down into produce categories, it is relatively simple to read-off the appropriate values from a stepped-graph, such as that shown in Figure 4.5.

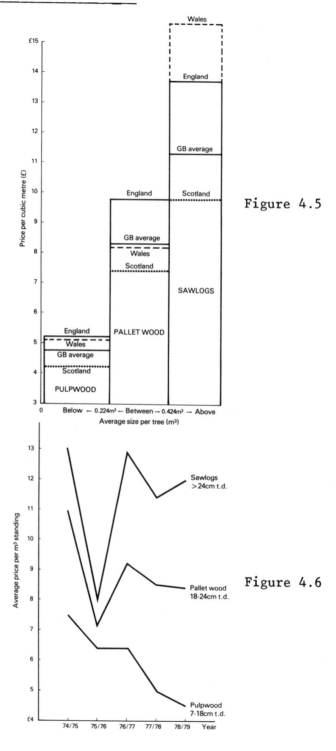

Figure 4.5

Figure 4.6

For example, if a certain stand containing $100m^3$ has $50m^3$ of pulpwood, $30m^3$ of pallet wood and $20m^3$ of saw-logs, the appropriate price from the graph can be multiplied by the volume in that category e.g.

Pulpwood	$50m^3$ x £ 4.74*	= £ 237.00
Pallet wood	$30m^3$ x £ 8.26	= £ 247.80
Saw logs	$20m^3$ x £11.29	= £ 225.80
	Total value of stand	£ 710.60

* These are the Great Britain average prices

The proportion of the volume in each produce category can again be obtained by using the Assortment Tables in the Forestry Commission's "Forest Management Tables".

It is also useful to use these produce categories to compare variations in price over a number of years. Figure 4.6 shows how these prices have varied over the five years from 1974/75 to 1978/79. From this graph, it can be seen quite clearly that prices, reflecting demand, have fallen over the period. This is particularly evident in the smaller sizes of roundwood, and the differential between pulpwood and saw logs has become exaggerated. The demand for saw logs has been much steadier and, in fact, prices have appreciated slightly.

4.6 Historical price-trends and the effects of inflation.

One of the great attractions of forestry to investors, such as Pension Fund managers, is that it is virtually inflation-proof. The trees keep appreciating in value as they grow, whatever the value of money.

If costs and prices keep largely in step, inflation may be ignored.

If the general level of world timber prices, since the turn of the Century, is studied it can be seen that, in real terms, these prices have appreciated slightly. Significantly, there is a difference between the three produce categories already described, namely pulpwood, pallet wood and saw logs.

The general level of prices for saw logs has appreciated at a rate of 2% compound interest in real terms. The pallet wood category, in this case including pit props, has increased at about 1.5% and pulpwood at about 1%. Thus the differential between the smaller and larger categories has steadily widened, relecting the short-term pattern in Figure 4.6.

The prices for small-sized round wood are continuing to fall, in relation to the larger sizes, and this has been further affected by pulp and chipboard manufacturers using more industrial waste - such as sawdust and offcuts - instead of round wood.

There will obviously be local demands for small material in intensive agricultural and horticultural areas, but these are not likely to affect the overall pattern. Certain temporary demands, such as for motorway fencing materials, also occur but fluctuate very rapidly.

Since all future prices are unknown, it is only possible to make forecasts by using inspired guess-work backed by a reasonable interpretation of past trends. In the economists phrase "all things being equal", in the light of past trends and the likelihood of future supply and demand, it would be reasonable to suppose that prices will continue to appreciate in real terms at these levels.

Chapter 5

5.1   Volume Yield Tables

Since the early 19th Century, Volume Yield Tables
have been used for forest management purposes. They
are, in fact, statements of the expected volume production at various ages throughout the life of a crop.
Usually, such tables show separately the volume in the
"main crop" and "thinnings".

The rate of growth of different stands of trees
varies considerably from one to another, depending on
species, site and genetic origin. To draw up a yield
table, it is necessary to classify stands in some way
so that they may be more easily related one to another.

The earliest yield tables, developed in Germany and
Austria, were based on the concept of "Quality Class".
This depended on the height reached by the 100 largest
trees at a certain age. Taking 50 years as the standard, Quality Class I Scots pine reached 70 feet at
that age while Quality Class IV only reached 40 feet.
Separate yield tables were then drawn-up for each
species and quality class.

The first yield tables produced by the Forestry Commission in Britain in 1920 were based on this principle.

These tables were revised in 1946, using data collected from many hundreds of measurements in sample plots
all over the country during the intervening years.
However, the Quality Class system had many draw-backs,
particularly since it was not easy to relate one species to another as Quality Class I of one species could
have a lower yield than Quality Class IV of another.

So in 1966 the Forestry Commission published a new
set of tables based on "Yield Class". This represented the maximum Mean Annual Increment of the stand and
is directly comparable whatever the species and when-
ever it reaches its maximum. The first set of tables
based on Yield Class was expressed in Imperial measure
(Hoppus feet per acre), but a new set of tables was
published in 1971 using metric units (cubic metres per
hectare) which has now been generally accepted in Britain. Yield Class 12 now means that the maximum Mean
Annual Increment of the stand is $12m^3$ per hectare per
annum.

Standard yield tables usually show a number of items
of information at each age represented, as well as the
volume yield. These include:

1. Number of trees per hectare
2. Mean breast-height diameter
3. Basal area per hectare
4. Mean height
5. Volume per hectare of the main crop
6. Volume per hectare of thinnings
7. Form factor
8. Mean Annual Increment and Current Annual
    Increment at that age

Volume yield tables can thus be used to forecast
production from a wood at various ages throughout the
life of the crop. Care has to be taken, however, to
ensure that the stocking and thinning treatment are
the same as those assumed in the table. Since very
rarely does an actual stand conform to a mathematical
model, such as a yield table, adjustments must be made
to allow for the difference.

However, used with care and making due allowances, Volume Yield Tables can be useful tools in forest management planning. For financial planning it is useful to have production expressed directly in money terms. The "Money Yield Table" is in fact a Volume Yield Table converted into money terms.

5.2   Money Yield Tables

The money yield from a stand of trees depends on the volume of timber produced and the price obtainable per cubic metre. The former can be obtained from a Volume Yield Table and the latter from a Price-size gradient, as described in Chapter 4.

If the average volume per tree can be calculated from the table, this can be directly related to the price per cubic metre, as shown by the graph. Then the total volume per hectare can be multiplied by the price to give the yield in money terms.

For this purpose, a graph such as that shown in Figure 4.3 can be used to relate the average volume per tree with the appropriate price per cubic metre. However, the price obtained in this way is not altogether reliable as it is quite possible that prices do not increase as steadily as the graph may indicate. Usually, prices go up in steps as the material passes from one category to another. The use of a "stepped graph" as shown in Figure 4.4 is probably more reliable.

This idea of classifying produce categories is not new. A Prussian forester, A. Schwappach, suggested such a method in 1908 based on the clearly defined timber classes then current in his country. He called this the "Method of Sortiments". Table 5.1 shows the classification and prices he used. His volume yield tables showed not only the total volume per hectare for the main crop and thinnings, but also the percentage in each "sortiment". From these figures he calculated a money yield table for each age.

The process described in Section 4.4, where three

Table 5.1

Prussian Timber "Sortiments"				
Timber	Class I	over 2 m³	22 marks per m³	
	II	1-2 m³	19 *"*	*"*
	III	0.5-1 m³	13 *"*	*"*
	IV	below 0.5 m³	10 *"*	*"*
Pit Wood			9 *"*	*"*
Firewood:	Split billets		7 *"*	*"*
	round-wood		4 *"*	*"*
	faggots		1 *"*	*"*

Table 5.3

AGE	VOLUME — MAIN CROP (m³)				VOLUME — THINNINGS (m³)				TOTAL VOLUME PER HECTARE
	7-18 cm.t.d.	18-24 cm.t.d.	>24 cm.t.d.	TOTAL	7-18 cm.t.d.	18-24 cm.t.d.	>24 cm.t.d.	TOTAL	
20	64	0	0	64	11	0	0	11	75
25	90	1	0	91	41	1	0	42	133
30	123	10	0	133	40	2	0	42	175
35	144	37	1	182	39	3	0	42	224
40	135	83	16	234	35	7	0	42	276
45	114	121	46	281	29	12	1	42	323
50	93	137	93	323	20	16	4	40	363
55	77	136	148	361	13	15	6	34	395
60	67	127	201	395	9	12	8	29	424

Table 5.4

AGE	VALUE — MAIN CROP (£)				VALUE — THINNINGS (£)				TOTAL VOLUME PER HECTARE
	£4.75	£8.30	£11.30	TOTAL	£4.75	£8.30	£11.30	TOTAL	
20	304	0	0	304	52	0	0	52	356
25	428	8	0	436	195	8	0	203	639
30	584	83	0	667	190	17	0	207	874
35	684	307	11	1002	185	25	0	210	1212
40	641	689	181	1511	166	58	0	224	1735
45	541	1004	520	2065	138	100	11	249	2314
50	442	1137	1051	2630	95	133	45	273	2903
55	366	1129	1672	3167	68	125	68	261	3428
60	318	1054	2271	3643	43	100	90	233	3876

"produce categories" - Pulpwood, pallet wood and saw
logs - are used is merely a development of the same
idea. The Forestry Commission's "Management Tables"
give volume yield tables by species and yield class.
Table 5.2 shows that for Sitka spruce Yield Class 12.
From this it can be seen that separate volumes are
given for the categories 7cm, 18cm and 24 cm top diameter, which are roughly equivalent to the three produce categories mentioned.

To make the task of constructing a money yield table
easier, it is necessary to slightly recast the information given in the Forestry Commission's Normal Yield
Table. As it stands, the volume given in the 7cm
column, in fact, includes the volumes in the other two
columns. This is obvious enough when you think that
if it is over 18 or 24cm, it is also over 7cm. The
7cm column includes the total volume over 7cm. Table
5.3 shows the figures in Table 5.2 adjusted so that
the volumes are given in the three categories:

   7 - 18cm,   18 - 24cm   and over 24 cm.

To get these figures, the volume in the 24cm category
has to be deducted from that in the 18cm category, and
the figure in the 18cm category from that in the 7cm
category. These volumes now correspond reasonably
closely to the three produce categories.

From the "stepped graph", Figure 4.4, the prices for
the three categories are read-off as:

         Pulpwood (7 - 18cm) £4.75
         Pallet
             wood (18 - 24cm) £8.30 and
         Saw logs (over 24cm) £11.30

It is then a simple matter to convert the volumes into
values by using these prices. Table 5.4 shows a money
yield table constructed from the information in Table
5.3, using these prices from Figure 4.4.

Step-by-step, the procedure is illustrated as
follows:-

Table 5.2

Sitka Spruce
Normal Yield Table: Yield Class 12

	MAIN CROP After Thinning							Yield From THINNINGS						CUMULATIVE PRODUCTION		INCREMENT			
					Volume in cubic metres to top diameters of:						Volume in cubic metres to top diameters of:					C.A.I.		M.A.I.	
Age	Number of Trees	Top Ht.	Mean Diam.	Basal Area	7 cm	18 cm	24 cm	Number of Trees	Mean Diam.	Mean Vol. per	7 cm	18 cm	21 cm	Basal Area	Vol. to 7cm	Basal Area	Vol. to 7cm	Vol. to 7cm	Vol. Age
		m	cm	m²					cm	m³				m²	m³	m²	m³	m³	
(1)	(2)	(3)	(4)	(5)	(6)	(7)	(8)	(9)	(10)	(11)	(12)	(13)	(14)	(15)	(16)	(17)	(18)	(19)	
20	3079	7.7	10.2	25.0	64	0	0	131	13.0	0.087	11	0	0	26.8	75	2.34	11.8	3.7	20
25	2149	10.2	12.0	24.2	91	1	0	930	12.8	0.045	42	1	0	38.0	144	2.12	15.3	5.8	25
30	1584	12.7	14.5	26.1	133	10	0	565	13.5	0.074	42	2	0	47.9	228	1.86	17.5	7.6	30
35	1206	15.1	17.3	28.3	182	38	1	378	14.7	0.111	42	3	0	56.6	320	1.62	18.5	9.1	35
40	956	17.4	20.1	30.5	234	99	16	250	16.6	0.168	42	7	0	64.1	413	1.39	18.3	10.3	40
45	785	19.4	22.8	32.1	281	167	46	171	18.8	0.245	42	13	1	70.5	503	1.18	17.2	11.2	45
50	664	21.2	25.3	33.3	323	230	93	121	21.0	0.333	40	20	4	76.0	585	1.00	15.5	11.7	50
55	585	22.7	27.4	34.6	361	284	148	79	23.0	0.428	34	21	6	80.5	657	0.81	13.6	11.9	55
60	529	23.9	29.3	35.7	395	328	201	56	24.7	0.521	29	20	8	84.3	720	0.70	11.7	12.0	60
65	487	25.0	30.9	36.6	423	365	248	42	26.3	0.615	26	19	9	87.5	774	0.59	10.2	11.9	65
70	455	25.9	32.4	37.4	447	396	289	32	27.6	0.709	23	18	10	90.3	821	0.52	9.0	11.7	70
75	429	26.7	33.6	38.1	469	423	323	26	28.9	0.793	21	17	10	92.7	864	0.45	7.9	11.5	75
80	407	27.3	34.7	38.6	486	444	351	22	30.0	0.871	20	17	11	94.7	901	0.38	6.4	11.3	80

At age 35

Main crop $\begin{array}{ll}(7 - 18\text{cm}) & = & 144\text{m}^3 \text{ x } \pounds\ 4.75 & = & \pounds\ 684 \\ (18 - 24\text{cm}) & = & 37\text{m}^3 \text{ x } \pounds\ 8.30 & = & \pounds\ 307 \\ (\ \ - 24\text{cm}) & = & 1\text{m}^3 \text{ x } \pounds 11.30 & = & \pounds\ \ 11\end{array}$

Total, maincrop: £1002

Thinnings $\begin{array}{ll}(7 - 18\text{cm}) & = & 39\text{m}^3 \text{ x } \pounds\ 4.75 & = & \pounds\ 185 \\ (18 - 24\text{cm}) & = & 3\text{m}^3 \text{ x } \pounds\ 8.30 & = & \pounds\ \ 25 \\ (\ \ - 24\text{cm}) & = & 0 \ \ \text{ x } \pounds 11.30 & = & \pounds\ \ \ 0\end{array}$

Total, thinnings: £ 210

Total value at age 35 = £1212 per hectare

This procedure is repeated on each line to give the total value per hectare at that age. In this way the whole table is built up so that the value per hectare of the main crop and thinnings may be directly read-off for any age from 20 to 60 years. It should be noted that the timber value before 20 years is "nil".

5.3 Using the Money Yield Table

One of the commonest uses for a Money Yield Table is for the purpose of valuation. Woods have to be valued for various reasons, such as for sale, purchase, pro-bate, taxation and for management purposes.

If money yield tables are available for various species and yield classes, it is a simple process to carry out a quick valuation. If the stands are grouped by species, yield class and age, the value per hectare from the money yield table can be multiplied by the appropriate area to give the total value. To take a simple example, where the woods are all of the same species and yield class (Sitka spruce yc 12), but of different ages, the figures from Table 5.4 can be used as follows:-

10 yrs.	20 hectares	x	nil		nil
15 yrs.	5 "	x	nil		nil
25 yrs.	10 "	x	£ 639 per ha.		£6,390
35 yrs.	10 "	x	£1212 " "		£12,120
40 yrs.	20 "	x	£1735 " "		£34,700
50 yrs.	25 "	x	£2903 " "		£72,575
60 yrs.	10 "	x	£3876 " "		£38,760
	100 hectares				£164,545

This gives the "Realisation Value" of the wood, if
it is felled and sold there and then.

Where different species and yield classes are present, money yield tables would have to be available for
each. However, in most commercial woods the number of
species does not exceed about six, and the number of
yield classes per species is often not more than three
or four, so the number of tables to be used will be
limited.

Money yield tables can also be used to forecast
future values. If the purpose is to build up a
reserve of capital, then it can be seen by calculations, as above, when the total value of the woods
reaches the desired amount.

The relative values of different crops, of different
species and yield classes, can be compared in the same
way. This could also give an indication of the relative productivity, in money terms, of different sites
capable of growing trees of various species and yield
classes.

For purposes of financial management, money yield
tables are a useful source of information. The next
chapter deals with the processes of compounding and
discounting to give present values of future benefits
and debt, using money yield tables as a base. However,
there is one such calculation that can be made directly

from the money yield table, without compounding or
discounting. This is where the value of the current
annual increment is expressed as a percentage of the
value of the growing stock, to give the current annual
value increment percent (£CA1%), sometimes called the
"Indicating Percent".

Taking the figures from Table 5.4 and considering
the current annual increment between the ages of 35
and 40, the percentage value can be calculated as
follows:-

Total Value per hectare at age 40 =   £ 1735
                         at age 35 =   £ 1212

    Value increment over 5 yrs. =   £ 523

Average annual increment 523 ÷ 5 =   £ 104.60

Average value of Growing Stock over the
period - £ 1735 + 1212 ÷ 2 = £ 1473.50

Current Annual Value Increment percent

$$= £ \frac{104.60}{£1473.50} \times 100 = 7.1\%$$

If a series of such calculations is made, over the
life of a crop, a point can be seen where this percentage drops below an acceptable level. At this
point, felling and replacement of the crop has to be
considered. (See Chapter 9).

Chapter 6

6.1   Present value of future receipts.

The Money Yield Tables, discussed in the previous
chapter, give the expected value per hectare of the
crop at the age stated. This is useful information
when dealing with crops which are at that age, but
often it is necessary to look at the present values
of future receipts from the start of the rotation.

This can be done by taking the value per hectare at
each age in the Money Yield Table and discounting
that value back to the beginning of the rotation.
When all these values have been discounted back to the
same point in time, they are fully comparable. It can
be seen, at a glance, the age at which the crop reaches
the maximum discounted revenue.

If the values in the Money Yield Table are plotted
against age on a graph, the curve shows a steady increase over the rotation. This is shown in Figure
6.1. However, if the discounted revenues are plotted
in the same way, the curve rises to a peak and then
drops away, as shown in Figure 6.2. This is because,
after this point, any increase in value becomes in-
creasingly offset by the effects of discounting over a
longer period. The rate of discounting used makes a

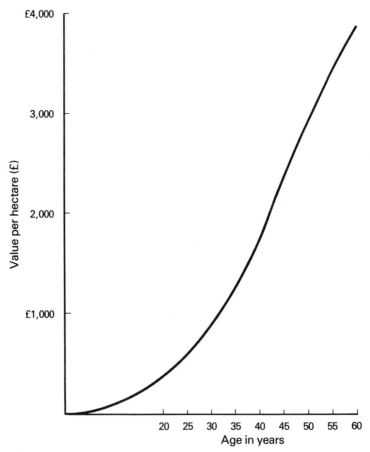

Figure 6.1

great difference to the age at which the revenue
reaches its maximum. The higher the rate, the earlier
it culminates and vice-versa.

Discounted revenue tables can be constructed from
the money yield tables and used to compare the relative returns from different species and yield classes.
One particular species and yield class may give a
higher value yield, but take longer to reach it. In
this case, a lower return on a shorter rotation may in
fact be more rewarding financially.

6.2   Constructing a Discounted Revenue Table.

Using the Money Yield Table (Table 5.4) as a basis,
a Discounted Revenue Table can be constructed by
applying the appropriate discount factor at each age.
In Table 6.3, columns 1, 3 and 5 have been transferred
directly from Table 5.4. The appropriate discount
factors, at 5%, for each age are shown in column 2.

By multiplying the actual values in columns 3 and 5
by the discount factor in column 2, the discounted
values are obtained and entered in columns 4 and 6.
To take into account previous revenues from thinnings,
their discounted values are accumulated in column 7.
This means that the discounted values of thinnings at
a particular age (column 6) are added to the previous
figure in column 7 to give the accumulated total at
that age. So the total discounted value at any age
includes that of the main crop (column 4) and the
accumulated value of thinnings to that date (column
7) to give the total figure in column 8.

This accumulation process takes into account not
only the value of the main crop at that particular age
but also the benefits of previous intermediate returns
from thinnings. When over a rotation, often more than
half the total yield - both in volume and money terms
- comes in the form of thinnings, it would be wrong
not to make due allowance for this income.

From this table (Table 6.3) it can now be seen that
the maximum discounted revenue for this crop, at 5%

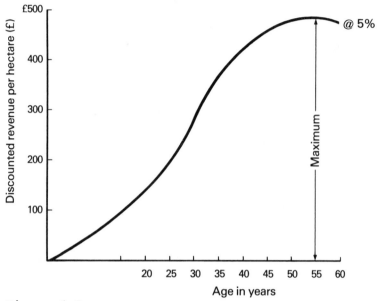

Figure 6.2

Table 6.3

AGE	DISCOUNT FACTOR @ 5%	MAIN CROP		THINNINGS			TOTAL DISCOUNT VALUE PER HA.
		Actual Value	Dis- counted Value	Actual Value	Dis- counted Value	Accum- ulated Dis- counted Value	
(1)	(2)	(3)	(4)	(5)	(6)	(7)	(8)
20	0.377	304	115	52	20	20	135
25	0.295	436	129	203	60	80	209
30	0.231	667	154	207	48	128	282
35	0.181	1002	181	210	38	166	347
40	0.142	1511	215	224	32	198	413
45	0.111	2065	229	249	28	226	455
50	0.087	2630	229	273	24	250	479
55	0.068	3167	215	261	18	268	483
60	0.054	3643	197	233	13	281	478

discount rate, comes at 55 years where the figure is
£483 per hectare. After this age, the total discounted revenue starts to drop and the longer it is delayed, the less will be the total return on the plantation. At a lower rate of discount, the maximum
occurs later and at a higher rate it comes earlier.
Figure 6.4 shows the effects of 3%, 5% and 7% discount
rates.

6.3 Compounded revenue and discounted revenue.

So far, we have been looking into the future from a
viewpoint at the beginning of the rotation. This is
the standpoint from which comparisons have to be made
when deciding on a course of action to be taken, such
as which species to plant or how much to pay for the
land. However, sometimes it is necessary to consider
the position at the end of a rotation or at some point
in the middle. In such a situation, it has to be remembered that in order to bring all receipts to the
same point in time, those in the past have to be compounded and those in the future have to be discounted.

Taking the figures from Table 5.4 and considering
the position at age 40, the receipts in years 20, 25,
30 and 35 have to be compounded for 20, 15, 10 and 5
years. The receipts at age 40 would be the actual
figure and those for 45, 50, 55 and 60 years would
have to be discounted for 5, 10, 15 and 20 years.
These values have now all been brought to the same
point, age 40 years, and can be added to give the
total value at that age.

If the position at the end of the rotation were to
be considered, then all the receipts would have to be
compounded for the appropriate number of years up to
60 years. An alternative approach would be to discount all receipts to the beginning of the rotation,
add them together and then compound the total to which
ever age is to be considered. This avoids having to
discount some receipts and compound others but some
errors will creep in with the double multiplication,
unless the factors are taken to five or more places
of decimals.

6.4   Present value of future (or past) expenditure.

To get a true reflection of the profitability of a woodland area, expenditure as well as revenue must be taken into account. In forestry, most expenditure occurs early in the rotation with ground preparation, planting and establishment forming the greater part of the cost. Beating-up and weeding can continue over the next few years, with cleaning and brashing taking place later still. Road-making, ideally, should be left until just before the roads are likely to be needed. In any case, there is an argument that the full cost should not be charged against a single rotation as the roads, once constructed, will be used for several rotations. In which case such charges could be capitalised and only part charged against one rotation, depending on the expected life. Annual maintenance charges, for drains and fence upkeep, protection can also be capitalised.

To be able to relate revenue and expenditure, occurring at different times, both must be brought to the same point in time by discounting or compounding. If all revenues have been discounted to the start of the rotation, the same must be done for expenditure. Similarly, if all receipts have been compounded to the end of the rotation, costs must be dealt with in the same way.

To show that the same effect results from either discounting or compounding, the following example has been completed both ways:-

Year	Amount	Discount Factor		Discounted Expenditure
0	£ 500	x1.00	=	£ 500.00
5	£ 50	x0.784	=	£ 39.20
10	£ 100	x0.614	=	£ 61.40
				£ 600.60

x18.679 (compounded 60 yrs)
= £11,219.90

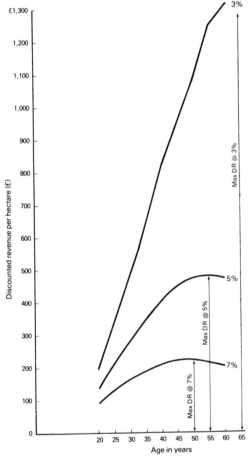

Figure 6.4

Table 6.5

Age	DISCOUNT FACTOR		MAIN CROP			THINNINGS					TOTAL	
	3%	7%	Actual value	Dis-t counted @ 3%	Dis- counted @ 7%	Actual value	Dis- counted @ 3%	Dis- counted @ 7%	Accumu- lated 3%	Accumu- lated 7%	3%	7%
20	0.554	0.258	304	168	78	52	29	13	29	13	197	91
25	0.476	0.184	436	208	80	203	97	37	126	50	334	130
30	0.412	0.131	667	275	87	207	85	27	211	77	486	164
35	0.354	0.093	1002	355	93	210	74	20	285	97	818	190
40	0.307	0.067	1511	464	101	224	69	15	354	112	818	213
45	0.263	0.047	2065	543	97	249	66	12	420	124	960	221
50	0.228	0.034	2630	600	89	273	62	9	482	133	1082	222
55	0.196	0.024	3167	620	76	261	51	6	533	139	1153	215
60	0.170	0.017	3643	619	62	233	40	4	593	143	1212	205

Years Compounded	Compound Factor		Compounded Expenditure
60	x18.679	=	£9339.50
55	x14.673	=	£ 733.65
50	x11.467	=	£1146.70
			£11,219.85

x0.0535 (discounted 60 yrs)
= £ 600.60

So the results are the same whether it is discounted back and then compounded forward, or vice-versa.

6.5 Costs of operations.

Just as in constructing the price/size gradient in Chapter 4, the Forestry Commission schedules of prices for standing sales of timber were used as a basis, so for calculating discounted expenditure it is possible to use the standard costs published from time to time. These are not generally available from the Forestry Commission but are shown in a booklet published by C. E. Hart called "British Timber Prices and Forestry Costings".

Obviously, these costs will vary considerably from place to place, depending on the different conditions and methods of work. However, an average level of expenditure can be estimated from these figures and used in such calculations.

The following examples give an indication of such costs Hart (1979):-

1. Land purchase:
       £350 - £400 per hectare

2. Ground preparation:
       Scrub-cutting £75 - £800 per hectare.
       Hand-turfing £40 - £60 per hectare.
       Ploughing (shallow) £60 - £100 per hectare.

2. Ground preparation: contd.
     Ploughing (deep) £90 - £125 per hectare.

3. Draining:
     New drains (by hand) £50 - £100
       "   "   (by machine) £30 - £45

     (assuming 200-300 metres per hectare)

4. Fencing:
     Rabbit fencing   £1.75 per m.
     (Strengthened for sheep)   £2.25 per m.
     Stock fencing   £3.00 per m.
     Deer fencing   £5.00 per m.

5. Planting:
     Mattock £8 - £12 per thousand plants
     Notching £10 - £20 per thousand plants
     Planting on ploughed ground £5 - £10 per
                  thousand plants.
     Tubed seedlings £3 - £5 per thousand plants.
     Pit planting £25 - £30 per thousand plants.
     Screefing and notching £15 - £30 per
                  thousand plants.

6. Purchase of plants:
     These can vary from £15 per thousand for
                  1 year seedling conifers to
                  £400 - £500 per thousand for
                  unrooted poplar sets.

7. Weeding:
     Hand weeding £30 - £100 (soft grasses to
                  woody weeds)
     Chemical £20 - £45)
     Mechanical £10 - £45) Prices per hectare)
     Aerial spraying £60 - £70 Prices per hectare.

8. Maintenance:
     Drains maintenance (by hand) £5 - £15 per
                  hectare.
     Fences maintenance   20p per metre.

9. Brashing:
  £35 (larch) to £90 (Sitka spruce) per hectare.

10. Pruning:
  2 to 4m height 6p to 10p per tree
  4 to 6m height 8p to 12p per tree
  6 to 7m height 4p to 8p per tree
  Total (3 stages) 18p to 30p per tree

11. Cleaning:
  By hand £35 - £60 per hectare
  Chemical £25 to £50 per hectare

12. Thinning:
  First thinning (conifers) £3.75 to £7.50 per m^3
  First thinning (hardwoods) £4.00 to £7.50 per m^3
  Subsequent (conifers) £3.50 to £7.50 per m^3.
  Subsequent (hardwoods) £4.00 to £7.75 per m^3.

13. Felling:
  Large conifers £1.50 to £2.05 per m^3.
  Large hardwoods £2.00 to £2.75 per m^3.

14. Extraction:
  Skidders 1.5 to 15.5m^3 per hour
  Forwarders 5.0 to 8.0m^3 " "
  Cable cranes 2.5 to 4.0m^3 " "
  Processors 2.7 to 25.0m^3 " "

  Average costs per m^3 are likely to be between
  £1 and £3.50.

15. Conversion:
  Cross-cutting and stacking £1 to £1.50 per m^3
  Peeling (machine)   £1 to £1.50 per m^3
  Pointing (sawbench)   2p to 3p per stake
  Splitting (ripping)   £1 to £1.05 per m^3

16. Haulage:
  From £2 (30km) to £4.50 (110km) per tonne

Overall cost of establishment (Private forestry)

(a) Mainly conifers:

	England and Wales		Scotland
	Mainly small areas - lowland	Mainly extensive upland areas	Mainly extensive upland areas
	£800 per ha.	£430 per ha.	£330 per ha.

(b) Mainly broadleaved trees:
In this case the cost is likely to be £150 per ha. more than for conifers.

		(Forestry Commission)
England	(Average)	£365 per ha.
Wales		£445 per ha.
Scotland		£315 per ha.

Chapter 7

7.1   Net present value.

If all the costs of establishing and maintaining a
plantation are discounted back to the beginning of
the rotation and deducted from the sum of all receipts
which have been similarly treated, the result is the
net present value. This is usually expressed as a sum
of money per unit area at a particular rate of compound interest (say £150 per hectare @ 5%).

This figure gives the net present value of the investment, or of the site, which can be compared with
other investments or sites. It also indicates whether
such an investment would make a profit or a loss at a
particular rate of interest. If money had to be borrowed at a higher rate, it would be likely that a loss
would occur. If money can be borrowed at a lower rate
then the profit is likely to be that much higher.

In doing such calculations, it is important to
ensure that all costs and receipts are expressed as
present values at a common point in time. This is
usually by discounting to the start of the rotation
but can also be done by compounding to the end. It
is only when this has been done that they are truly
comparable and can be added together or subtracted one

from the other.

The net value, whichever way it has been obtained,
is a useful yardstick by which to compare one course
of action with another. It can show, for example,
how much could be paid for the land to make a profit,
break-even, or make a loss. It also shows how much
expenditure can be afforded, at various stages, related to the expected returns.

7.2   Soil Expectation Value.

This term, used by many early forest economists, is
a misleading translation of the German expression
"Bodenerwartungswert", which would be better described as "land" or "site" expectation value. It is
obtained by compounding costs to the end of the rotation, deducting them from the receipts and then
discounting the result back to the start of the rotation.

The German forester, Martin Faustmann, devised a
formula for calculating the soil expectation value -
usually known as the "Faustmann Formula".

$$S = \frac{Yr + \Sigma Ta.1.0p^{r-a} - C.1.0p^n}{1.0p^r - 1} - \frac{e}{.0p}$$

Where S is the soil expectation value; Yr the yield
at the end of the rotation 'r'; $\Sigma Ta.1.0p^{r \cdot a}$ the
yield from all the intermediate thinnings, each compounded to the end of the rotation; $C.1.0p^n$ the costs
compounded to the end of the rotation; $1.0p^r - 1$ the
discounting factor back to the beginning; $\frac{e}{.0p}$ the
capitalised annual maintenance charges.

Since this was in the days before electronic pocket
calculators were in general use, working out the formula was a tedious business. So to make matters easier
a set of "multipliers" were devised for each expression in the formula for various rotations. These were
set out in a series of tables so that the appropriate
multipliers could be read-off against the appropriate
number of years for various rates of compound interest.

Table 7.1 shows a calculation of the soil expectation value based on the figures in the Money Yield Table (Table 5.4) and the appropriate Faustmann multipliers.

7.3   Net Discounted Revenue (NDR).

Today, rather than go through the complicated procedure of using the Faustmann multipliers to get the soil expectation value, it is more usual to use the net discounted revenue (NDR). This is the discounted revenue less the discounted expenditure (NDR: DR-DE).

Instead of the complexity of compounding everything to the end of the rotation and then discounting it back to the beginning, everything is directly discounted in the first place.

From Table 6.3 it can be seen that the maximum discounted revenue, at 55 years, is £483. If the discounted expenditure is taken as being £400, the net discounted revenue is £83 per hectare @ 5%. DR (£483) − DE (£400) = NDR (£83).

If this NDR figure is compared with the soil expectation value, calculated in Table 7.1, it can be seen that they are not quite the same. In the first place, the soil expectation value was based on a 60 year rotation, while the NDR was calculated on a 55 year rotation. If the NDR were based on a 60 year rotation, it is reduced to £78 per hectare, compared with the soil expectation value of £63. This difference lies in the fact that in the case of NDR it has only been discounted over one rotation, while the soil expectation value is discounted "in perpetuity" over many rotations. This is because the classical continental foresters usually thought in terms of a "normal" forest continuing over a great number of rotations while today it is treated as a one-off exercise. However, the NDR is a useful "tool" in decision-making and its use is discussed further in a later section.

7.4   NDR Calculations

Table 7.1

Operation/ Year	Actual Figures	Faustmann Multiplier	Compounded/ Discounted sum
Y60	£3643	× 0.057	£207.65
T20	52	× 0.400	20.80
T25	203	× 0.310	62.93
T30	207	× 0.240	49.68
T35	210	× 0.190	39.90
T40	224	× 0.150	33.60
T45	249	× 0.120	29.88
T50	273	× 0.090	24.57
T55	261	× 0.070	18.27
TOTAL RECEIPTS			487.28
C	£400	× 1.06	424.00
SOIL EXPECTATION VALUE			£63.28

Table 7.2

Year	Discount Factor @5%	DISCOUNTED REVENUE (DR)					TOTAL DR	DISCOUNTED EXPENDITURE (DE)					(DR-DE) NDR
		MAIN CROP		THINNINGS				Operation	Cost	Dis-counted	Accumu-lated	
		Sale price	Dis-counted	Sale price	Dis-counted	Accumu-lated						
(1)	(2)	(3)	(4)	(5)	(6)	(7)	(8)	(9)	(10)	(11)	(12)	(13)
0	1.000							Planting	250	250	250	− 250
1	0.952							BU/weeding	75	74	324	− 324
2	0.907							Weeding	30	28	352	− 352
3	0.864											
4	0.823											
5	0.784											
10	0.614											
15	0.481							Brashing	100	48	400	− 400
20	0.377	304	115	52	20	20	135					− 265
25	0.295	436	129	203	60	80	209					− 191
30	0.231	667	154	207	48	128	282					− 118
35	0.181	1002	181	210	38	166	347					− 53
40	0.142	1511	215	224	32	148	413					+ 13
45	0.111	2065	224	249	28	226	455					+ 55
50	0.087	2630	229	273	24	250	479					+ 79
55	0.068	3167	215	261	18	268	483					+ 83
60	0.054	3643	197	233	13	281	478					+ 78

To calculate the net discounted revenue (NDR) it is necessary to obtain the discounted revenue (DR) and the discounted expenditure (DE). These are shown in the previous chapter (6.2 and 6.4).

For convenience, a composite proforma can be used on which all the calculations are shown (Table 7.2). On this form, both discounted revenues and discounted expenditures are calculated. The difference between them gives the net discounted revenue. The discounted revenue, including accumulated thinnings, for each age is shown in column (8). The discounted expenditure in column (12) is deducted from the discounted revenue to give the net discounted revenue in column (13).

From this table it is now possible to see, at a glance, which is the rotation of maximum NDR at that particular rate of interest. If the calculations are repeated for a number of different rates of interest, their effects on the net return can be seen. This will be dealt with further under the section on the Internal Rate of Return.

In Table 7.2, discounted expenditure at various ages have been accumulated in column (12), so that a direct relationship can be made with the accumulated discounted revenue. It must be emphasised that the NDR is a sum of money per unit area (£/Ha) at a particular rate of interest. It is not itself a percentage rate.

7.5   Uses and limitations of NDR

The main drawback to the use of net discounted revenue is that it depends on an arbitrary rate of interest. The apparent profitability, or otherwise, of a project can depend solely on the rate of interest used.

However, whatever the rate of interest used, the relative positions remain the same over the length of a normal forest rotation. It may be a case of seeing which is the least unprofitable but at least the ranking order of various proposals can be determined.

Where other factors are constant, it is quite realistic to use NDR to compare one species of tree-crop with another or to measure the performance of a species of one Yield Class with that of another. It is also possible to compare the relative profitability of a low-yielding species of early culmination of increment - such as larch - with another higher yielding species of late culmination - such as Norway spruce. The time -span can have a marked effect in such cases.

It is possible to use NDR in determining how much can be paid for the land on which a crop is to be planted. If the maximum discounted revenue is known, then the balance left after deducting all other discounted expenditure is what can be used to pay for the land and still break-even. If the land can be bought for less than this price, then a profit can be made. One can argue that the value of the land will remain the same - or even in times of inflation increase - so that the value at the end of the rotation will cancel out the original cost.

Similar calculations can be made to see how much can be spent on ground preparation or in applying fertilisers. Obviously, if a higher financial return can be obtained as a result of such work, then provided the discounted extra expenditure does not exceed the extra discounted revenue, it is worthwhile.

NDR calculations can also be used to decide on the optimum financial rotation and when is the best time to replace an uneconomic crop with a more profitable one.

These and other ways of using NDR calculations are described in further detail in later chapters where examples are given. A word of caution should be added that such calculations can only be a guide and cannot guarantee certainty. Price/size gradients and money yield tables only give the position at the present time. No one can say for certain what markets and prices will be like at any time in the future. A demand for previously unsaleable material may suddenly develop or a type of produce, now much in demand, could become unsaleable.

Within these limitations and provided that such calculations are used as a relative guide, they can be a useful tool for making decisions.

Chapter 8

8.1   The effects of various compound interest/discount
rates on net discounted revenue.

Table 7.2 shows the effect of NDR calculations,
using a 5% discount rate, where the maximum NDR on a
55 year rotation works out at + £83 per hectare. If
other discount rates are used, the results vary considerably from + £812 per hectare @ 3% to - £178 per
hectare @ 7%. So the profitability, or otherwise, of
a project can depend entirely on the rate of interest
used.

As has already been explained, NDR can be used per-
fectly satisfactorily to compare the relative profitability of two courses of action where conditions are
generally similar. This would be the case where the
performance of two different tree species, or yield-
classes of the same species, on the same site are to
be compared.

Where the relative profitability of two quite different projects are to be compared - say forestry and
hill-farming - then it is more useful to be able to
compare the actual rate of return of the projects
independant of arbitrarily chosen interest rates. In
other words, the interest generated by the projects

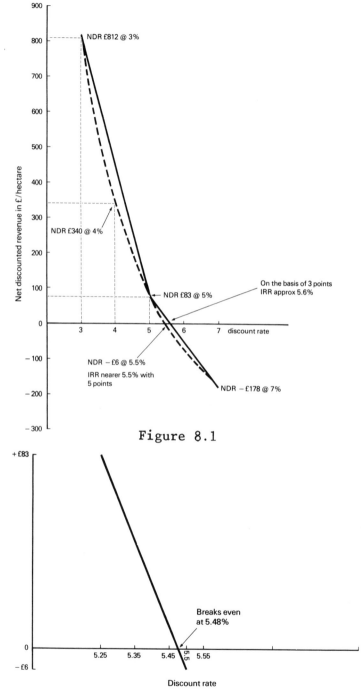

Figure 8.1

Figure 8.2

themselves.

For this purpose, a useful yardstick is the internal
rate of return (IRR). This is the break-even point,
where, at a particular rate of interest, the discounted revenue equals the discounted expenditure. So,
IRR is that rate of compound discount at which DR = DE
or where DR - DE = 0.

Taking the figures at the beginning of this section,
@ 5% the NDR is + £83 and @ 7% it is - £178. So it
would be reasonable to suppose that at a rate of interest somewhere between 5% and 7%, the NDR would be zero.
That rate of interest would be the internal rate of
return.

8.2   Calculating the IRR by graphical methods.

If the three figures, already mentioned, of NDR @ 3%,
5% and 7%, namely + £812, + £83 and - £178, are plotted
on a graph (Figure 8.1) it can be seen that the line
joining these points cuts the zero line at 5.6%. This
is the approximate value of the IRR.

This is an approximation only, because these points
are really on a curve and not on a straight line. To
get a more accurate figure, it is necessary to plot
intermediate values at 5.25%, 5.5% and 6%. Figure 8.2
shows the curve resulting from plotting these extra
points and the IRR is now more accurately shown as
5.48%.

While an approximate value of the IRR can be obtained with three points, bracketed on either side of the
expected value, for a more accurate figure it is necessary to use more points. Since each point on the
graph is the result of elaborate NDR calculations, it
can be a tedious task. However, it is not often necessary to determine the IRR to that degree of accuracy.
In most cases a value to the nearest 0.5% is near
enough and for this purpose, three points @ 4%, 5% and
6% will suffice. The first approximation @ 5.6%, if
taken to the nearest 0.5% and the more accurate 5.48%,
rounded-up, would both end up at 5.5%.

To calculate the IRR, by the graphical method
requires that at least three sets of NDR calculations have to be made as on Table 7.2 for three
different discount rates. Care has to be taken in
choosing the most suitable rates with which to calculate as otherwise some distortion in the line can
occur if they are too far apart. If the approximate
IRR can be judged, then rates as near as possible
and on either side of the final figure can be chosen.
However, the graphical method can be a tedious process
if many points have to be calculated and some other
method may be preferred.

8.3 Calculating the IRR by the formula method.

Calculating the IRR by the graphical method described in the previous section can be very tedious
if a lot of points on the curve have to be determined.
Another method of arriving at the IRR is to use the
formula:

$$ \sqrt[n]{\frac{R}{E}} \quad - \quad 1 \quad x \quad 100 \quad = \quad IRR $$

Where R = actual receipts; E = actual expenditure
and n = number of years.

Taking the Projects A, B and C in Chapter 2, the
IRR for each can be simply determined by using the
formula as follows:

Project A: Receipts £400; expenditure £100; number of years 15.

$$n\sqrt{\dfrac{R}{E}} - 1 \times 100 = 15\sqrt{\dfrac{400}{100}} - 1 \times 100 = 15\sqrt{4} - 1 \times 100 = 1.0968 - 1 \times 100$$

$$= 0.0968 \times 100 = 9.68\%$$

Project B: Receipts £500; expenditure £100; number of years 25.

$$25\sqrt{\dfrac{500}{100}} - 1 \times 100 = 25\sqrt{5} - 1 \times 100 = 1.0664 - 1 \times 100 = 0.0664 \times 100$$

$$= 6.64\%$$

Project C: Receipts £1000; expenditure £100; number of years 50.

$$50\sqrt{\dfrac{1000}{100}} - 1 \times 100 = 25\sqrt{10} - 1 \times 100 = 1.0471 - 1 \times 100 = 0.0471 \times 100$$

$$= 4.71\%$$

These results may be compared with those calculated
by the graphical method in Section 3.1.

The use of this sort of formula has been inhibited
in the past by the calculation of the nth root by
arithmetical means. Nowadays, with electronic pocket
calculators commonly in use, these calculations are
not so daunting.

The examples just given for the use of the formula
are straight forward as the expenditure and receipts
all occurred at the beginning or end of the period of
time. In forestry, however, this is not usually the
case as has been described already. The use of the
formula is only possible if all receipts can be taken
to the end and all expenditure to the beginning of a
project. This can be done by compounding all receipts
to the end and discounting all expenditure to the beginning. However, in doing so an arbitrary compound
interest rate has to be introduced, which was intended
to be avoided. If a rate somewhere near the expected
IRR is used, this will not distort the calculations
too much.

If the maximum discounted revenue from Table 7.2
(£483) is taken and compounded to the end of the rotation (55 years) @ 5%, it comes to £7,069 (£483 x 14.
636). If this figure and the discounted expenditure
(£400) are used in the formula, the IRR works out at
5.365%.

$$\sqrt[55]{\frac{7069}{400}} \;-\; 1 \;\times\; 100 \;=\; 5.365\%$$

This gives a slightly lower figure than that obtained by the graphical method (5.48%) but if rounded up
would still come to 5.5%. This is a much quicker way
than the tedious business of having to calculate a
number of values of NDR to plot on a graph and is probably sufficient for general purposes.

8.4 Uses for the IRR in Forest Management.

The IRR is the best measure to use when comparing the

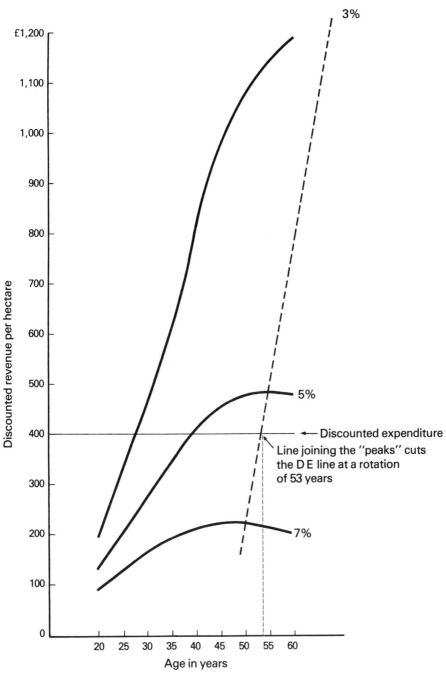

Figure 8.3

profitability of forestry with quite dissimilar investments. For example, where forestry can produce a
return of 5.6% compared with, say, hill sheep farming
at 5% or a grouse moor at 8%. This is much more easily
appreciated than NDR calculations at various rates of
interest, producing pssibly negative results. Such
figures can also be compared with industrial or commercial investments and show immediate advantages or
disadvantages.

8.5 Using IRR to determine optimum length of rotation.

From Tables 6.3 and 6.5, it could be seen that the
rotations of maximum discounted revenue (and hence net
discounted revenue) varied from 60 + years at 3%, to
55 years at 5% and 50 years at 7%. Thus the length of
rotation depended on the arbitrary test rate. So perhaps a better yardstick might be to look for the rotation of maximum internal rate of return.

Table 8.4 shows a practical method of finding the
IRR at various ages of the crop over its rotation. At
each age shown, at five-year intervals, the IRR is calculated using the formula method already described.
To the actual value of the main crop, obtained from the
money-yield table, must be added the accumulated value
of the thinnings to that age. This is done by taking
the accumulated discounted value of the thinnings and
compounding them up the appropriate number of years.
The total revenue at that age is then divided by the
discounted expenditure and applied to the formula.

Column (8) of Table 8.4 shows the IRR for each age
and in Column (9) the NDR is shown as a comparison.
When this is plotted on a graph (Figure 8.5) it can be
seen that the rotation of maximum IRR is about 50 years.
Since we have already determined that the IRR is about
5.4% (5.38), we would expect the rotation at that rate
to be slightly shorter than at 5% (55 years). In fact
as the calculations have been made at five year intervals, it is not possible to get the rotation to an
intermediate year.

Using the figures from Tables 6.3 and 6.5, plotting

Table 8.4

Age 'n'	Actual Value Main Crop	Accum-ulated Discount Value Thin-nings	Com-pounded Acc.D.V. Thin-nings	Total (2)+(4)	(5) ÷ DE	$\sqrt[n]{(6)}$	IRR	NDR @5%
(1)	(2)	(3)	(4)	(5)	(6)	(7)	(8)	(9)
20	304	20	53	357	0.890			
25	436	80	271	707	1.767	1.029	2.90	− 191
30	667	128	553	1220	3.050	1.038	3.80	− 118
35	1002	166	916	1918	4.795	1.046	4.60	− 53
40	1511	198	1393	2904	7.260	1.0508	5.10	+ 13
45	2065	226	2030	4095	10.237	1.0530	5.30	+ 55
50	2630	250	2866	5496	13.740	1.0538	5.38	+ 79
55	3167	268	3922	7089	17.723	1.0536	5.36	+ 83
60	3643	281	5248	8891	22.228	1.0530	5.30	+ 78

Explanation:

On each line —
Column (1):   Age (number of years)
(2):   Actual value of main crop at that age (col.(3). Table 6.3)
(3):   Accumulated Discounted Value of thinnings (Col.(7). Table 6.3)
(4):   Column (3) × 1.05^n (where 'n' is the age in Col.(1))
(5):   Total revenue ÷ column (2) + column (4)
(6):   Total revenue ÷ discounted expenditure: column (5) ÷ 400
(7):   'n'th root of figure in column (6) — where 'n' is age in column (1)
(8):   IRR = (Column (7) − 1) × 100
(9):   NDR in column 13 of Table 7.2

N.B. Figures in Column (8) are plotted against ages in Column (1) in Figure 8.

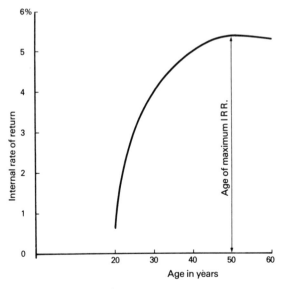

Figure 8.5

them against age, joining the culmination points with a straight line and drawing a horizontal line for the discounted expenditure, we see that the line cuts at 53 years which is in fact the rotation of maximum IRR. (Figure 8.3).

Optimum replacement age can also be determined, as discussed in the next chapter, by relating IRR to the indicating percent.

Where the NDR is a negative figure, it has little meaning when comparing it with other negative figures or even positive ones. In such cases, the IRR is a better comparison. For example: At 5%, the NDR for three different species and yield classes are:-

A. Oak (Yield Class 6)   = - £369 (DR £131 - DE £500) 70 yrs.

B. Scots pine (Yield Class 8)   = - £112 (DR £238 - DE £350) 80 yrs.

C. Douglas fir (Yield Class 14)   = + £413 (DR £813 - DE £400) 50 yrs.

Except that @ 5% a lot of money will be lost on oak and Scots pine and make a reasonable profit on Douglas fir, it is difficult to compare their performances directly. If the IRR is calculated by the formula method the results are more easily compared.

Since the discounted revenues have been calculated at 5%, it is possible to find the actual revenue by compounding at 5% over the rotation.

$$\textbf{A. } 131 \times 1.05^{70} = 131 \times 30.426 = \left(70\sqrt{\dfrac{3986}{500}} - 1\right)100$$

$$= \underline{3.01\%} \text{ (IRR)}$$

B. $238 \times 1.05^{80} = 238 \times 49.561 = \left(\sqrt[80]{\dfrac{11,795}{350}} - 1\right)100$

$$= \underline{4.5\%} \; (\text{IRR})$$

C. $813 \times 1.05^{50} = 813 \times 11.467 = \left(\sqrt[50]{\dfrac{9,323}{400}} - 1\right)100$

$$= \underline{6.5\%} \; (\text{IRR})$$

So it is now possible to see that Douglas fir (Yield Class 14) has a potential rate of return of more than twice as much as the oak (Yield Class 6). It is also possible to see at a glance that while Scots pine produces a loss @ 5% it would make a profit @ 4%.

IRR figures can also be used to compare the effects of various treatments of the crop, such as ground preparation, fertiliser application, thinning regimes and fluctuations in the market.

Chapter 9

9.1 The Indicating Percent.

The Indicating Percent, or more accurately the
Current Annual Value Increment Percent (£CAI%), shows
the rate at which the value of a plantation, wood, or
forest increases in a year in comparison with the
value of the growing stock. This has already been
described in Chapter 5 (Section 5.3) where a simple
example was given. The formula used for this calculation is:

$$\frac{V^2 - V^1}{V^2 + V^1 \div 2} \quad x \quad 100$$

Where V^1 is the value at the first measurement and
V^2 is the value at the second. The difference between
the two is the value of the increment and the sum of
them both divided by 2 gives the average value of the
growing stock. If the period between the two measurements is more than a year, the value of $V^2 - V^1$ will
have to be divided by the number of years to give the
annual figure.

Table 9.1 shows a series of such figures over a rotation taken from the Money Yield Table (Table 5.4) and
these are plotted on a graph in Figure 9.2.

Table 9.1

	Present Main Crop + Thinnings	Earlier Main Crop – Thinnings	Average Annual Increment	Agerage Growing Stock	£CAI %
Age	V^2	V^1	$\dfrac{V^2 - V^1}{5}$	$\dfrac{V^2 + V^1}{2}$	$\dfrac{I}{GS} \times 100$
(1)	(2)	(3)	(4)	(5)	(6)
25	639	304	67	471.5	14.20
30	874	436	87.6	655.0	13.37
35	1212	667	109	939.5	11.60
40	1735	1002	146.6	1368.5	10.71
45	2314	1511	160.6	1912.5	8.40
50	2903	2065	167.6	2484.0	6.75
55	3428	2630	159.6	3029.0	5.27
60	3876	3167	141.8	3521.5	4.03

Column (1) Age at which calculation is to be made.
       (2) V^2 Present main crop (including thinnings)
       (3) V^1 Previous main crop (5 years earlier) less thinnings
       (4) Average annual value increment over the five years.
       (5) Average value of Growing Stress over the five years.
       (6) The Indicating per cent.

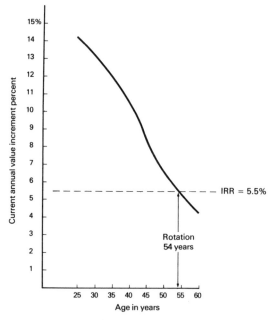

Figure 9.2

From previous calculations, in Chapter 8, it was
shown that the IRR for such a stand of Sitka spruce
(Yield Class 12) is 5.5%. From Figure 9.2 it can be
seen that the Indicating Percent falls below 5.5%
between 50 and 55 years. This also ties-in with the
length of rotation determined by other methods.

The great advantage of the Indicating Percent is
that it does not depend on historical costs or future
expectations. No compound interest rates are involved
and it is based on actual figures based on two measurements. It is of the greatest value when dealing with
a mature stand for which no records are available.

If the IRR is known, or can be estimated, it is
simply a matter of seeing if the Indicating Percent is
higher or lower than this figure. If it is lower, the
stand should be felled. If it is higher, it can be
safely left for a period before felling, after a further measurement.

9.2 Optimum replacement date.

When deciding whether an existing crop should be replaced by another, the criterion usually used is when
the sum of the discounted revenue (DR) of the existing
crop and the net discounted revenue (NDR) of the successor crop is at a maximum:

$$\max_{\geq} \quad DR^e + NDR^s$$

It should be remembered that looking at it from the
present moment, any delay in felling the existing crop
also delays the ultimate return on the successor crop.
So, the increase in value of the existing crop has to
be sufficient to offset the drop in value of the successor crop through waiting.

Table 9.3 shows the relevant figures for the example
already discussed and Figure 9.4 shows them plotted on
a graph.

If a relatively uneconomic crop, say Sitka spruce
Yield Class 12, is to be replaced by a more productive

Table 9.3

Age	DR^e	NDR^s	$DR^e + NDR^s$	
0	25	83	108	
5	33	65	98	
10	42	51	93	e = existing crop
15	53	40	93	s = successor crop
20	135	31	166	
25	209	26	235	
30	282	19	301	
35	347	15	362	
40	413	12	425	
45	455	9	464	
50	479	7	486	
55	483	6	489	← Maximum*
60	478	5	483	

$\Sigma^{max}DR^e + NDR^s = £489$
(55yrs)*

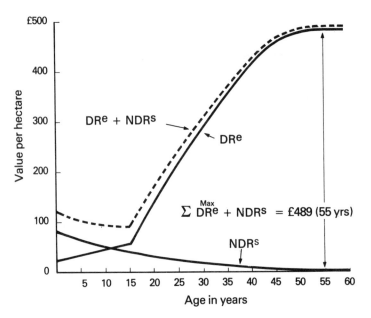

$$\Sigma \overset{Max}{DR^e} + NDR^s = £489 \text{ (55 yrs)}$$

Figure 9.4

one, say Douglas fir Yield Class 14, a series of such calculations can show the best time to make the change. A series of such calculations is shown in Table 9.5 and plotted on a graph in Figure 9.6. From these it can be seen that unless the replacement takes place very early in the rotation (ideally before the uneconomic species was planted), it is better to wait until the first crop reaches somewhere near its maximum.

A lot will also depend on the point in the rotation at which the calculation is made. If it is near the beginning, what has just been said will apply. However, if it is later on, the optimum time bay be before the culmination of the existing crop. This can be seen clearly from the graph in Figure 9.7.

9.3   Return on Capital invested.

Investors and financiers are particularly interested to know the return on the capital invested. For this purpose, the tools already described may be used in a number of ways to give the information required.

(a)   Financial Yield: The Internal Rate of Return (IRR) is also known as the financial yield and gives the return in percentage terms - e.g. 5.5% for Sitka sprcue (Yield Class 12) in the example given.

(b)   Yield per Unit Area: The Net Discounted Revenue (NDR) gives the return in the form of a sum of money per unit area at a particular rate of interest - e.g. £83 per hectare @ 5% over a 55 year rotation.

(c)   Benefit/Cost Ratio: This gives the ratio between the benefit - i.e. the discounted revenue and the cost - i.e. the discounted expenditure. - e.g. in the example £483 ÷ £400 = £1.21. This means that for every £1 invested, there is a return of £1.21, or a net return of 21p.

Table 9.5

	Age	From Year '0'			From Year 20		From Year 30	
		DR^e	NDR^s	$DR^e + NDR^s$	NDR^s	$DR^e + NDR$	NDR^s	$DR^e + NDR^s$
Considered from	0	25	413	438				
3 points in time:	5	33	334	367				
Year 0, Year 20	10	42	254	296				
and Year 30.	15	53	199	252				
	20	135	156	291	413	548		
	25	209	122	331	334	543		
	30	282	96	378	254	536	413	<u>695</u>
	35	347	75	422	199	546	334	681
	40	413	59	472	156	569	254	667
	45	455	46	501	122	<u>577</u>	199	654
	50	479	36	<u>515</u>	96	575	156	635
	55	483	28	511	75	558	122	605
	60	478	22	500	59	537	96	574

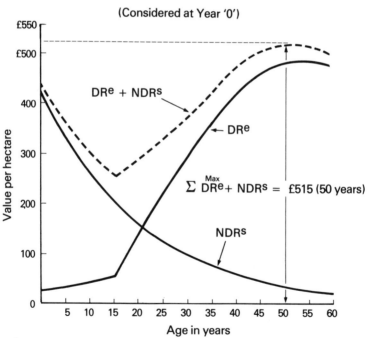

(Considered at Year '0')

$DR^e + NDR^s$

DR^e

$$\sum \overset{Max}{DR^e} + NDR^s = \text{£515 (50 years)}$$

NDR^s

Value per hectare

Age in years

Figure 9.6

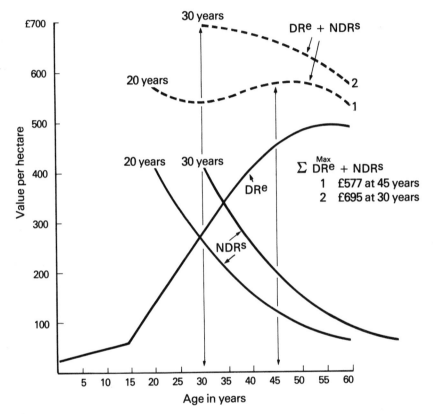

Figure 9.7

(d) <u>Production Cost per m^3</u>: If the compounded ex-
     penditure is divided by the total volume of
     timber produced, the cost per m^3 is obtained.
     This would be the sale price needed per m^3 to
     break even; e.g. £400 x 14.6356 = £5,854 ÷ 395
     m^3 = £14.82 per m^3.

Chapter 10

10.1   To plant, or not to plant, trees?

In many cases, the decision to plant trees depends
on factors other than financial ones. It may be decided on the fact that a regular supply of timber is
needed to supply a sawmill, that fencing materials are
needed for estate repairs or that the woods are needed
for shelter or for amenity.

However, if it is to be a straight forward financial
choice between forestry and some other land-use, such
as sheep farming, then a comparison of their relative
rates of return can be a help.

For example, if it is known that on a particular
hillside sheep farming can provide a return of 6% but
also that it is capable of growing Sitka spruce (Yield
Class 18), which is the more profitable course of
action?

To find this out, it is necessary to calculate the
Internal Rate of Return (IRR) of Sitka spruce (Yield
Class 18). This can be done by using the "formula
method" described in Chapter 8 (Section 8.3). The
formula is:

$$n\sqrt{\frac{R}{E}} - 1 \times 100 = IRR.$$

Table 10.1

| AGE | MAIN CROP | | | | THINNINGS | | | | TOTAL |
	7cm	18cm	24cm	TOTAL VOLUME	7cm	18cm	24cm	TOTAL VOLUME	TOTAL VOLUME
15	74	0	0	74	1	0	0	1	75
20	99	2	0	101	61	2	0	63	164
25	134	20	0	154	59	4	0	63	217
30	131	79	14	224	53	10	0	63	287
35	101	130	66	297	37	22	4	63	360
40	74	132	156	362	24	27	12	63	425
45	55	111	250	416	15	24	23	62	478
50	42	93	332	467	9	16	28	53	510

Table 10.2

| AGE | MAIN CROP | | | | THINNINGS | | | | TOTAL |
	£4.75	£8.30	£11.30	TOTAL £ m.c.	£4.75	£8.30	£11.30	TOTAL £ THIN-NINGS	£ per Ha.
15	352	0	0	352	5	0	0	5	357
20	470	17	0	487	290	17	0	307	794
25	637	166	0	803	280	33	0	313	1116
30	622	656	158	1436	252	83	0	335	1771
35	622	1079	746	2447	176	183	45	404	2851
40	351	1096	1763	3210	114	224	136	474	3684
45	261	921	2825	4007	71	199	260	530	4537
50	200	772	3752	4724	43	133	316	492	5216

Table 10.3

| AGE | MAIN CROP | | | THINNINGS | | | Total |
	Discount Factor	Actual Value	Dis-counted Value	Actual Value	Dis-counted Value	ACC. D.V.	Dis-counted Value
15	0.481	352	169	5	2	2	171
20	0.377	487	184	307	116	118	302
25	0.295	803	237	313	92	210	447
30	0.231	1436	332	335	77	287	619
35	0.181	2447	443	404	73	360	803
40	0.142	3210	456	474	67	427	883
45	0.111	4007	445	530	59	486	931
50	0.087	4724	411	492	43	529	940

Max DR = £940
Less DE = 400
NDR = £540

Max DR 50 years

Tables 10.1, 10.2 and 10.3 give the relevant information for Sitka spruce (Yield Class 18). The maximum
discounted revenue (£940) is compounded @ 5% to the
end of the rotation (50 years) to give the value of
'R': £940 x 11.4567 = £10,779. If 'E' is taken as
being £400 as before, then the IRR is calculated:

$$50\sqrt{\frac{10,779}{400}} - 1 \times 100 = 6.8\%$$

From this it would appear that growing Sitka spruce
on this site would be marginally more profitable. If
only Yield Class 12 could be grown, with an IRR of
5.6%, then sheep farming would be marginally more profitable than forestry.

10.2   How much to pay for the land?

Traditionally, forest economists have tended to
think of the NDR as representing the value of the
site, as shown by the "soil" expectation value and
Faustmann's formula. This is to say that if the cost
of the land were included in the discounted expenditure and the project broke-even in financial terms, it
would mean that it had just made the rate of interest
used in the discounting calculations. In these circumstances, up to the amount of the net discounted
revenue could be paid for the land in the first place
and still break-even. If less than this were paid for
the land, there would be a surplus at the end. If
more had to be paid, there would be a deficit.

However, looking at it this way obscures an important fact. Unlike the money spent on establishment and
maintenance; which is really an operational cost, the
value of the land at the end of the rotation - in real
terms - remains the same. In fact, in some circumstances, the value could be higher as for example in
the case of reclamation work after open-cast mining.

So it could be said that the land value is the true
capital involved, while the other is in fact "working"
capital. In which case the NDR represents the return

on the land value.

If in the case of the crop of Sitka spruce (Yield Class 12) previously mentioned, where the NDR was £83, the land had cost £350 per hectare one could say that the actual return was $\frac{83}{350}$ x 100 or 23.7%.
Consequently one could pay up to four times as much as the NDR for the land and still make a reasonable return. (83 x 4 = £322).

Whichever way one looks at it, it is true to say that one can afford to spend more on good land, with high productivity, than on poor land with low productivity. Of course, poor land could be bought cheaply and perhaps improved to get higher productivity. This aspect will be dealt with in a later chapter.

10.3 What species of tree to plant?

Generally speaking, the choice as to which species of tree to plant will depend on silvicultural rather than on financial criteria. There is obviously no point in planting a species that will not grow well on the site. At the same time, economics and market factors will also have a bearing on the decision, for there is little point in planting a particular species - however well it grows - if there is no demand for its timber. All other things being equal, the choice should be made for the crop that gives the highest net discounted revenue.

Where two or more species apparently grow equally well, each of the same Yield Class, the financial return expressed by the NDR can be quite different. This depends on the pattern of growth and the age of culmination of mean annual increment.

For example, if on the same site Sitka spruce, Douglas fir and European larch can all achieve Yield Class 12, which would give the highest NDR? It is shown in Table 7.2 that Sitka spruce of this Yield Class gives an NDR of £83 per hectare (@ 5% on a 55 year rotation). Tables 10.4 to 10.6 and 10.7 to 10.9

Table 10.4

| AGE | MAIN CROP | | | | THINNINGS | | | | TOTAL |
	7cm	18cm	24cm	TOTAL VOLUME	7cm	18cm	24cm	TOTAL VOLUME	TOTAL VOLUME
10	27	—	—	27	—	—	—	—	27
15	67	1	—	68	18	—	—	18	85
20	84	14	—	98	41	1	0	42	140
25	78	50	10	138	34	8	0	42	180
30	58	78	43	179	21	17	4	42	221
35	41	76	98	215	12	18	12	42	257
40	30	63	155	248	7	13	20	40	288
45	23	51	204	278	4	4	23	36	314

Table 10.5

| AGE | MAIN CROP | | | | THINNINGS | | | | TOTAL £ per Ha. |
	£4.75	£8.30	£11.30	TOTAL £ m.c.	£4.75	£8.30	£11.30	TOTAL £ THIN-NINGS	
10	128	—	—	128	—	—	—	—	128
15	318	8	—	326	86	—	—	86	412
20	399	116	—	515	195	8	—	203	718
25	370	415	113	948	162	66	—	228	1176
30	276	647	486	1409	100	141	45	286	1695
35	195	630	1107	1932	57	149	136	342	2274
40	143	523	1752	2561	33	108	226	367	2928
45	109	423	2305	2837	19	75	260	354	3191

Table 10.6

| Age | Discount Factor | MAIN CROP | | THINNINGS | | ACC. D.V. | Total Discounted Value |
		Actual Value	Discounted Value	Actual Value	Discounted Value		
10	0.614	128	81	—	—	—	81
15	0.481	326	157	86	41	41	198
20	0.377	515	194	203	77	118	312
25	0.295	948	280	228	67	185	465
30	0.231	1409	326	286	66	251	577
35	0.181	1932	350	342	62	313	663
40	0.142	2561	364	367	52	365	729
45	0.111	2837	315	354	39	404	719

Max DR = £729
Less DE =   400
NDR   = £329

Max DR 40 years

Table 10.7

| AGE | MAIN CROP | | | | THINNINGS | | | | TOTAL |
	7cm	18cm	24cm	TOTAL VOLUME	7cm	18cm	24cm	TOTAL VOLUME	TOTAL VOLUME
20	75	—	—	75	20	—	—	20	95
25	106	5	—	111	42	—	—	42	153
30	129	27	—	156	39	3	—	42	198
35	111	74	16	201	35	7	—	42	243
40	81	106	58	245	25	15	2	42	287
45	57	102	124	283	16	19	7	42	325
50	42	84	190	316	10	17	15	42	358
55	32	70	246	348	6	11	20	37	385
60	26	59	294	379	4	7	21	32	411

Table 10.8

| AGE | MAIN CROP | | | | THINNINGS | | | | TOTAL |
	£4.75	£8.30	£11.30	TOTAL £ m.c.	£4.75	£8.30	£11.30	TOTAL £ THIN-NINGS	£ per Ha.
20	356	—	—	356	95	—	—	95	451
25	504	42	—	546	200	—	—	200	746
30	613	224	—	837	185	25	—	210	1047
35	527	614	181	1322	166	58	—	224	1546
40	385	880	655	1920	119	125	23	267	2187
45	271	847	1401	2519	76	158	79	313	2832
50	200	697	2147	3044	48	141	170	359	3403
55	152	581	2780	3513	29	91	225	345	3858
60	124	490	3322	3936	19	58	237	314	4250

Table 10.9

| AGE | MAIN CROP | | | THINNINGS | | | Total |
	Discount Factor	Actual Value	Dis-counted Value	Actual Value	Dis-counted Value	ACC. D.V.	Dis-counted Value
20	0.377	356	134	95	36	36	170
25	0.295	546	161	200	59	95	256
30	0.231	837	193	210	49	144	337
35	0.181	1322	239	224	41	185	424
40	0.142	1920	273	267	38	223	496
45	0.111	2519	280	313	35	258	538
50	0.087	3044	265	359	31	289	554
55	0.068	3513	239	345	23	312	551
60	0.054	3936	213	314	17	329	542

Max DR = £554
Less DE =   400
NDR   = £154

← Max. DR 50 yrs

give similar information on European larch and Douglas
fir of the same Yield Class. These figures show that
European larch has an NDR of £329 (40 years) and Douglas fir an NDR of £154 (50 years). While the Douglas
fir has a higher total volume production (588m³ per
ha.) than European larch (474m³ per ha.), the earlier
culmination of the latter has a considerable effect on
the discounted revenue. Consequently, only if the
Douglas fir could achieve a higher Yield Class - say
16 - would it be financially more rewarding. Both
these species, in these circumstances, do better than
the Sitka spruce.

The cost of the land does not need to come into
these comparisons, because it would be the same whichever crop is planted. Where the cost of establishment
is the same, the comparative performance of the species can be measured by using Discounted revenue alone.

10.4 Yield Class and NDR.

It was shown in the previous section that different
species of the same Yield Class can produce strikingly
different NDR figures. For the same species, however,
there does appear to be a direct relationship between
Yield Class and NDR. Previous figures quoted from
Tables 7.2 and 10.3 showed that for Sitka spruce Y.C.
12 the NDR was £82 and for Y.C.18 £540 per hectare.
Tables 10.10 to 10.12 show that for Y.C.24 the figure
is £1,079 per hectare. These three points are plotted
on a graph in Figure 10.13 and produce a straight line.
By interpolation, the values of NDR for Sitka spruce
Yield Classes 12 to 24 appear to be as follows:

Y.C	NDR
12	80
14	240
16	400
18	540
20	700

Table 10.10

| AGE | MAIN CROP | | | | THININGS | | | | TOTAL |
	7cm	18cm	24cm	TOTAL VOLUME	7cm	18cm	24cm	TOTAL VOLUME	TOTAL VOLUME
10	32	—	—	32	—	—	—	—	32
15	96	—	—	96	38	1	—	39	135
20	139	18	—	157	80	4	—	84	241
25	134	90	18	242	69	15	—	84	326
30	94	140	99	333	42	34	8	84	417
35	63	124	230	417	23	35	26	84	501
40	43	94	350	487	12	25	45	82	569
45	32	71	446	549	6	15	51	72	621
50	26	55	525	606	4	9	50	63	669

Table 10.11

| AGE | MAIN CROP | | | | THININGS | | | | TOTAL |
	£4.75	£8.30	£11.30	TOTAL £ m.c.	£4.75	£8.30	£11.30	TOTAL £ THIN-NINGS	£ per Ha.
10	152	—	—	152	—	—	—	—	152
15	456	—	—	456	181	8	—	189	645
20	931	150	—	1081	380	33	—	413	1494
25	637	747	203	1587	328	125	—	453	2040
30	447	1162	1119	2728	200	282	90	572	3300
35	300	1029	2599	3928	109	290	294	693	4621
40	204	780	3955	4939	57	208	509	774	5713
45	152	589	5040	5781	29	125	576	730	6511
50	124	757	5933	6814	19	75	565	659	7473

Table 10.12

| AGE | MAIN CROP | | | THININGS | | | Total Discounted Value | |
	Discount Factor	Actual Value	Discounted Value	Actual Value	Discounted Value	ACC. D.V.		
10	0.614	152	93	—	—	—	93	
15	0.481	456	219	189	91	91	310	
20	0.377	1081	408	413	156	247	655	Max DR = £1479
25	0.295	1587	468	453	134	381	849	Less DE = 400
30	0.231	2728	630	572	132	513	1143	NDR = £1079
35	0.181	3928	711	693	125	638	1349	
40	0.142	4939	701	774	110	748	1449	
45	0.111	5781	642	730	81	829	1471	
50	0.087	6814	593	659	57	886	1479	Max DR 50 years

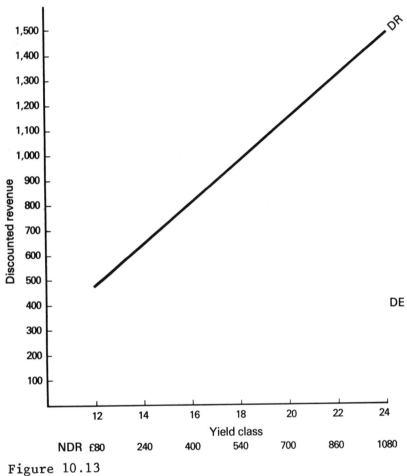

Figure 10.13

Y.C.	NDR
22	860
24	1080

The significance of this will be dealt with in later chapters when the effects of ground cultivation and fertiliser application are discussed. Obviously, if as a result of some improvement work the Yield Class can be raised, then the NDR will also be that much higher.

Chapter 11

11.1 Benefits of ploughing before planting.

Ploughing is usually carried out before planting to improve the drainage on a wet site, to prepare an easier surface on which to plant and to suppress the weeds. Since shallow ploughing for planting can cost something like £100 per hectare, the benefits must obviously be greater than this amount to make it worth while. Calculations must be made to relate costs to benefits in order to make the decision.

An example is given below in which two courses of action are considered:

(a) No ploughing:
2,500 Sitka spruce transplants (2 + 1) @ £50 per thousand = £125 per ha. Notching (planting) 2,500 @ £20 per thousand = £50 per ha. Weeding – 3 times @ £100, £80 and £80 per ha. Beating-up: Twice @ £60 per ha.

Year 1	Plants and planting	£175.00 x 1	£175.00
Year 2	Beating-up	£60 x 0.907	54.42
	Weeding	£100 x 0.907	90.70
Year 3	Beating-up	£60 x 0.863	51.83
	Weeding	£80 x 0.863	69.04

Year 4   Weeding   £80 x 0.822   £ 65.82

            Total discounted expenditure   £506.81

(b) With ploughing:
Ploughing @ £100 per hectare. 2,500 Sitka spruce
seedlings (2 + 0) @ £25 per thousand = £62.50
Planting - 2,500 @ £5 per thousand = £12.50
Beating-up (Year 2) @ £6 per hectare

Year 1   Ploughing £100 x 1   £100.00
         Plants and planting - £75 x 1   75.00
Year 2   Beating-up - £6 per hectare x
         0.907   5.42

            Total discounted expenditure   £180.42

In these circumstances, there is a saving of £326.39
per hectare, in spite of spending £100 per hectare on
ploughing, so it is obviously worth doing.

11.2   Applying fertiliser.

The expense of applying a fertiliser to a crop is
only justified if the financial benefit is greater than
the cost. This benefit can result from either shorten-
ing the rotation or increasing the yield. The following examples illustrate the point.

(a) If by the application of fertiliser, a crop of
     Sitka spruce (Yield Class 12) can be made to
     produce the same yield at 50 years instead of 55
     years, how much can be afforded to spend on the
     fertiliser?
     The maximum discounted revenue at 55 years for
     Sitka spruce (Y.C.12) is £483 per hectare (Table
     7.2). Since this has been discounted over 50
     years @ 5% it represents an actual figure of
     £7,069 (£483 x 14.636). If this figure is now
     discounted over only 50 years, the discounted
     revenue is now £616 (7,069 x 0.087). So the in-
     crease in discounted revenue is £133 (£616-483)
     and if the cost of applying fertiliser were no

Table 11.1

| AGE | MAIN CROP | | | | THININGS | | | | TOTAL |
	7cm	18cm	24cm	TOTAL VOLUME	7cm	18cm	24cm	TOTAL VOLUME	TOTAL VOLUME
15	39	—	—	39	—	—	—	—	39
20	75	—	—	75	27	1	—	28	103
25	106	3	—	109	48	1	—	49	158
30	137	22	—	159	46	3	—	49	208
35	138	69	10	217	42	7	—	49	266
40	115	117	42	274	34	14	1	49	323
45	90	136	99	325	24	20	5	49	374
50	71	131	169	371	16	20	9	45	416

Table 11.2

| AGE | MAIN CROP | | | | THINNINGS | | | | TOTAL £ per Ha. |
	£4.75	£8.30	£11.30	TOTAL £ m.c.	£4.75	£8.30	£11.30	TOTAL £ THIN-NINGS	
15	185	—	—	185	—	—	—	—	185
20	356	—	—	356	128	8	—	136	492
25	504	25	—	529	228	8	—	236	765
30	651	183	—	834	219	25	—	244	1078
35	656	573	113	1342	200	58	—	258	1600
40	546	971	475	1992	162	116	11	289	2281
45	428	1129	1119	3158	114	166	57	337	3495
50	337	1087	1910	3334	76	166	102	344	3678

Table 11.3

| Age | MAIN CROP | | | THINNINGS | | | Total Dis-counted Value | |
	Discount Factor	Actual Value	Dis-counted Value	Actual Value	Dis-counted Value	ACC. D.V.		
15	0.481	185	89	—	—	—	89	
20	0.377	356	134	136	51	51	185	
25	0.295	529	156	236	70	121	277	
30	0.231	834	193	244	56	177	370	
35	0.181	1342	243	258	47	224	467	
40	0.142	1992	283	289	41	265	548	
45	0.111	3158	351	337	37	302	653	Max DR
50	0.087	3334	290	344	30	332	622	

more than this it would at least break-even.

(b)   If by applying a fertiliser it is possible to
      raise the Yield Class of a crop of Sitka spruce
      from 12 to 14, is this worth doing if the cost
      of applying the fertiliser is £125 per hectare?

      The maximum discounted revenue for Sitka spruce
      (Yield Class 12) has already been mentioned as
      £483. From Table 11.1 it can be seen that for
      Yield Class 14 it is £653. The increase in dis-
      counted revenue by raising the Yield Class is
      thus £170 (£653-483). So, even by spending an
      extra £125 on applying fertiliser, there is a
      surplus of £45 over that for the original crop
      and so it would be worth doing.

11.3   Effects of windblow.

On some sites crops are unable to reach their full
potential yield as they are liable to windblow. If on
a particular site, crops are liable to be blown over
when their top height reaches 15m, a crop of Sitka
spruce (Yield Class 14) would reach this height at 30
years. It does not reach its maximum discounted revenue until 45 years. If the discounted revenue at
these two ages are compared, the loss due to premature
harvesting can be seen.

      Discounted revenue @ 45 years   =   £653
      Discounted revenue @ 30 years   =   £370
                                          ————
      Loss of revenue   =   £283
                                          ————

If by suitable deep draining it is possible to keep
the crop standing until it reaches age 45, then prov-
iding the cost of doing so does not exceed £283, it is
worth doing.

Alternatively, the use of a less-productive but more
windfirm species could be considered in the same way.
For example, if on the same site Sitka spruce (Yield
Class 18) and European larch (Yield Class 12) can be
grown but the spruce is likely to blow-over at 30 years

while the larch will stand, which is more profitable?

Discounted revenue Sitka spruce (Y.C.18) @ 30 years
= £619
Discounted revenue European larch (Y.C.12) @ 40 "
= £729

In these circumstances there is an argument to prefer the more windfirm species of lower yield than the other more susceptible species of higher potential but greater risk of windblow.

11.4   Erecting deer-fencing.

Similar calculations can be made to see whether it is worthwhile spending a lot of money on erecting deer-fencing. Obviously one has to compare costs and returns.

If by constant browsing of deer, a crop of Sitka spruce (Yield Class 18) is set-back 10 years and the maximum discounted revenue is not reached until 60 years after planting instead of 50 years, the maximum discounted revenue will be discounted over that further period.

Maximum discounted revenue at 50 years = £940
This represents an actual value of £10.779
(940 x 11.467)
Discounted over 60 years, this is £577 (10,779 x
.0533)

This is equivalent to a loss of discounted revenue of £363 per hectare (£940 - 577). So, if the cost of deer-fencing were less than this figure, it would be worthwhile. Instead of considering fencing, of course, a similar calculation could be done to justify the employment of a full-time keeper or ranger to control the deer.

11.5   Other establishment costs.

In the same way various other establishment techniques can be compared by relating their costs to the ex-

pected benefits. For example the use of larger plants,
which cost more and are more expensive to plant such
as "whips", can be justified if there is sufficient
saving in other costs, such as weeding and beating-up.
The discounted expenditure in each case can be compared to see which course of action gives the greater
benefit.

Chapter 12

12.1   Thinning, or a non-thinning regime?

From the volume yield table and the discounted revenue table for Sitka spruce (Yield Class 12), it can
be seen that, in both volume and money terms, thinnings contribute a large share in the total yield. In
fact the contribution in terms of discounted revenue
is far higher than that in terms of volume. This is
due to the effects of discounting where a smaller,
earlier return can be more valuable than a larger,
later return. In volume terms the final crop contributes 54% of the total and the thinnings 46%. In
terms of discounted revenue, the main crop contributes
43% and the thinnings 57%. This is on a 55 year rotation using a discount rate of 5%.

Generally speaking, within certain limits, the total
volume production from a stand is not greatly affected
by the number of trees per hectare. The same total
volume may be spread thinly over a larger number of
smaller trees, or thickly over a smaller number of
larger trees. However, where there is a large number
of small trees, many of them may be unsaleable or even
unmeasurable. The total "biomass" may be the same,
but the amount of timber of the sizes in demand will
be less.

Table 12.1

AGE	VOLUME				VALUE				Discount factor 25%	Discounted value (DR)
	7cm	18cm	24cm	TOTAL	£4.75	£8.30	£11.30	TOTAL		
20	71	—	—	71	337	—	—	337	0.377	127
25	135	4	—	139	641	33	—	674	0.295	199
30	200	20	—	220	950	166	—	1116	0.231	258
35	251	57	—	308	1192	473	—	1665	0.181	301
40	294	93	7	394	1397	772	79	2248	0.142	319
45	278	165	29	472	1321	1370	328	3019	0.111	<u>335</u> Max DR
50	244	227	69	540	1159	1884	780	3823	0.087	333
55	236	260	101	597	1121	2158	1141	4420	0.068	301
60	221	283	141	645	1050	2349	1593	4992	0.054	270
65	204	295	186	685	969	2449	2102	5520	0.042	232

Table 12.2

Age 55yrs	Orig. spacing	Nos. planted	Survivors	% age loss	7cm		18cm		24cm		TOTAL	
					Per ha. Vol(m^3)	%	Per ha. Vol(m^3)	%	Per ha. Vol(^{3})	%	Per ha. Vol(m^3)	%
	0.9m	12,345	2,278	82	424	75	134	24	10	1	568	100
	1.4m	5,102	1,913	63	297	52	225	39	53	9	575	100
	1.8m	3.086	1,385	55	236	40	260	44	101	16	597	100
	2.4m	1,736	1,018	41	126	23	213	39	212	38	551	100

Table 12.3

Age 55 yrs	7cm		18cm		24cm		TOTAL	
	Vol(m^3) per Ha	%	Vol(m^3) per Ha.	%	Vol(m^3) per Ha.	%	Vol(m^3) per Ha.	%
MAIN CROP	77	21	136	38	148	41	361	100
THINNINGS	228	77	56	19	11	4	295	100
TOTAL	305	47	192	29	159	24	656	100

Table 12.4

AGE	VOLUME (m³)				VALUE				Discount factor @5%	Discounted value (DR)
	7cm	18cm	24cm	TOTAL	£4.75	£8.30	£11.30	TOTAL		
20	63	—	—	64	304	—	—	304	0.377	115
25	90	1	—	91	428	8	—	436	0.295	129
30	123	10	—	133	584	83	—	667	0.231	154
35	144	37	1	182	684	307	11	1002	0.181	181
40	135	83	16	234	641	689	181	1511	0.142	215
45	114	121	46	281	542	1004	520	2066	0.111	229 Max DR
50	93	137	93	323	442	1137	1051	2630	0.087	229
55	77	136	148	361	366	1129	1672	3167	0.068	215

Table 12.5

Age	Discount Factor 5%	MAIN CROP		THINNINGS			Total
		Actual	Discounted	Actual	Discounted	Accumulated	
20	0.377	320	121	—	—	—	121
25	0.295	458	135	213	63	63	198
30	0.231	695	160	216	50	113	273
35	0.181	1027	186	219	40	153	339
40	0.142	1515	215	231	33	186	401
45	0.111	2044	227	252	28	214	441
50	0.087	2584	225	272	24	238	463
55	0.068	3101	211	251	17	255	466 Max DR
60	0.054	3562	189	229	12	267	456

In spite of the advantages of thinning already mentioned, in certain circumstances it may be preferable
to go in for a "non-thinning, clear-felling" regime.
This could be so where the market demand is for "cell-
ulose" rather than "timber" and the price/size gradient is level. If no higher price is paid for larger-
sized trees, then there is no point in producing them
and a large number of smaller trees would produce the
same volume and price.

As already discussed, this is not the position in
Britain today where the tendency has been for the
prices of larger-sized timber to remain steady, or
even appreciate, while small round-wood poles are be-
coming more difficult to sell. In these circumstances
there is obviously no advantage in not thinning, except for the possible difficulty in selling the thinnings!

There are also circumstances where a loss in total
saleable volume may be acceptable, if it can be offset
against savings in costs. For example, in the case of
a small isolated stand of trees where the costs of ex-
tracting and selling small parcels of thinnings may be
prohibitively high. Other circumstances could include
stands liable to windblow, where thinning would "let
in the wind", where a non-thinning, short rotation
clear-felling regime may be the only answer.

Table 12.1 shows the discounted revenues for a stand
of Sitka spruce (Y.C.12) which has not been thinned.
The 'standard' price/size gradient has been used for
this. This shows the maximum discounted revenue to be
£335 at 45 years compared with £487 at 55 years with
normal thinning. If the discounted expenditure were
the same as before - namely £400 - it would show a
loss of £65 per hectare compared with a gain of £87.

If the cost of extablishment could be reduced, perhaps by reducing the number of trees planted by using
wider spacing, it might be possible for the plantation
at least to break-even.

Work done by the Forestry Commission (Hamilton and

Table 12.6

Age	Volume (m³)				Value (£)				Discount factor	Discounted value
	7cm	18cm	24cm	TOTAL	£4.75	£8.30	£11.30	TOTAL	5%	(DR)
40	150	80	4	234	717	664	45	1426	0.142	203
45	156	146	22	281	741	1212	249	2202	0.111	244
50	174	204	46	323	827	1693	520	3040	0.087	264 Max D R
55	144	234	100	361	684	1942	1130	3756	0.068	255

Table 12.7

Year	No. of Trees	Price per Tree	Total Value	Discount Factor	Discounted Revenue
3	500	50p	250	0.864	216
4	1000	75p	750	0.822	617
5	1500	£1	1500	0.783	1175
6	2000	£1.25	2500	0.746	1865
7	1500	£1	1500	0.711	1280
TOTAL DISCOUNTED REVENUE					£5153

N.B. If this were combined with the return from the 'respaced' crop, the total Discounted Revenue would be £5417 per hectare.

Christie 1974) shows the effects of various original
spacings on non-thinned woods. Table 12.2 summarises
these findings for Sitka spruce (Y.C.12) at four different spacings between 0.9m and 2.4m. This shows that
at the wider spacing, while the total volume yield per
hectare is 105m^3 less than the normally thinned crop
(656-551), the proportion in the 18cm and 24cm categories is considerably higher - 425m^3 compared with
351m^3.

In these circumstances, if the price/size gradient
is such that the premium on larger sized trees is sufficient to cover the loss in total volume, then it
would be worth doing. If costs of extablishment are
also reduced, then it would be even more worthwhile.
However, this is not as simple as it may appear as
even if costs of plants and planting are reduced,
weeding, beating-up and maintenance could be higher.

12.2 "Thinning-to-waste" and "Respacing".

Where plantations have been established at normal
spacing and after establishment it becomes impossible
to sell small-sized thinnings, one answer to the problem of still producing sawlog-sized timber may be to
"thin-to-waste". This means that normal thinnings
would be undertaken but not harvested, leaving the
felled trees lying on the forest floor. Obviously,
no snedding or cross-cutting would be done. The
value of the thinnings would be lost and the costs
unrecovered, but the remaining trees would be free to
develop and produce saw-timber. Table 12.4 shows the
financial calculations for such a crop.

In some cases, where only the smaller-sized trees
are unsaleable, a first thinning would be done "to-
waste" and subsequent thinnings sold in the normal
way. This is then known as a "pre-commercial" thinning or in Britain as a "cleaning" or "de-wolfing".
Often this is combined with the removal of unwanted
broadleaved regrowth from stool-shoots. Table 12.5
shows an example where the first thinning is done non-
commercially and normal subsequent thinnings. There
is an obvious advantage here, especially if the "pre-

Table 12.8a

AGE	MAIN CROP				THINNINGS				TOTAL
	7cm	18cm	24cm	TOTAL VOLUME	7cm	18cm	24cm	TOTAL VOLUME	TOTAL VOLUME
20	64	—	—	64	11	—	—	11	75
25	91	—	—	91	42	—	—	42	133
30	129	4	—	133	41	1	—	42	175
35	161	22	—	183	37	5	—	42	225
40	150	80	4	234	27	14	1	42	276
45	135	127	20	282	20	19	3	42	324
50	110	162	52	324	14	20	6	40	364
55	119	194	83	396	—	—	—	—	396
60									

Table 12.8b

AGE	MAIN CROP				THINNINGS				TOTAL
	£4.75	£8.30	£11.30	TOTAL £ m.c.	£4.75	£8.30	£11.30	TOTAL £ THIN-NINGS	£ per Ha.
20	304	—	—	304	52	—	—	52	356
25	432	—	—	432	200	—	—	200	632
30	613	33	—	646	195	8	—	203	849
35	765	183	—	948	176	42	—	218	1166
40	713	664	45	1422	128	116	11	255	1677
45	641	1054	226	1921	95	158	34	287	2208
50	523	1345	588	2456	67	166	68	301	2757
55	565	1610	938	3113	—	—	—	—	3113
60									

Table 12.8c

AGE	MAIN CROP			THINNINGS			Total
	Discount Factor	Actual Value	Dis-counted Value	Actual Value	Dis-counted Value	ACC. D.V.	Dis-counted Value
20	0.377	304	115	52	20	20	135
25	0.295	432	127	200	59	79	206
30	0.231	646	149	203	47	126	275
35	0.181	948	172	218	40	166	338
40	0.142	1422	202	255	36	202	404
45	0.111	1921	213	287	32	234	447
50	0.087	2456	214	301	26	260	<u>474</u> Max DR
55	0.068	3113	212	—	—	260	472
60	0.054						

Table 12.9a

AGE	MAIN CROP				THINNINGS				TOTAL
				TOTAL				TOTAL	VOLUME
	7cm	18cm	24cm	VOLUME	7cm	18cm	24cm	VOLUME	
20	64	—	—	64	11	—	—	11	75
25	91	—	—	91	42	—	—	42	133
30	129	4	—	133	41	1	—	42	175
35	134	48	1	183	34	8	—	42	225
40	112	105	17	234	31	11	—	42	276
45	96	141	45	282	20	19	3	42	324
50	84	152	88	324	16	19	5	40	364
55	66	149	147	362	10	17	7	34	396
60	87	193	179	459	—	—	—	—	459

Table 12.9b

AGE	MAIN CROP				THINNINGS				TOTAL
				TOTAL £				TOTAL £	£ per Ha.
	£4.75	£8.30	£11.30	m.c.	£4.75	£8.30	£11.30	THIN-NINGS	
20	304	—	—	304	52	—	—	52	356
25	432	—	—	432	200	—	—	200	632
30	613	33	—	646	195	8	—	203	849
35	637	398	11	1046	162	66	—	228	1274
40	532	872	192	1596	147	91	—	238	1834
45	456	1170	509	2135	95	158	34	287	2422
50	399	1262	994	2655	76	90	57	223	2878
55	314	1237	1661	3212	48	141	79	268	3480
60	413	1602	2023	4038	—	—	—	—	4038

Table 12.9c

AGE	Discount Factor	MAIN CROP		THINNINGS		ACC. D.V.	Total Discounted Value
		Actual Value	Discounted Value	Actual Value	Discounted Value		
20	0.377	304	115	52	20	20	135
25	0.295	432	127	200	59	79	206
30	0.231	646	149	203	47	126	275
35	0.181	1046	189	228	41	167	356
40	0.142	1596	227	238	34	201	428
45	0.111	2135	237	287	32	233	470
50	0.087	2655	231	223	19	252	483
55	0.068	3212	218	268	18	270	488
60	0.054	4038	218	—	—	270	488

commercial" thinning is a fairly heavy "low" thinning.

A more recent development has been to carry-out "re-spacing". This is a "once-and-for-all" operation, carried-out early in the life of the crop - say just before canopy closure - to reduce the crop to final spacing. After this it is left alone until the final felling. The planting at normal spacing ensures that the trees are drawn-up, are free of side branches and herbaceous weeds are suppressed. It also provides more choice in the selection of final crop trees. After "respacing", the remaining trees have sufficient room to grow to final size. Table 12.6 shows possible financial returns from a "respaced" crop.

A variation of the "respacing" principle is employed in the system known as "Oceanic Forestry" advocated by Maj. Gen. D. G. Moore. Here, instead of cutting down the trees to be removed at ground level, they are "lopped" at about 1.4m above the ground. The idea behind this is to remove the competition from the final crop trees but, by allowing the severed trees to "bush-out", maintain ground cover between them. Other claims are also made about mycorrhizal benefits and that the slow suppression and death of the "lopped" trees being less harmful to the remaining trees than their sudden removal.

Other ways of dealing with the problem of unsaleable small thinnings include combining growing trees with a field crop. The trees are planted at final spacing in a matrix of some other agricultural crop - even potatoes! - which is removed before the tree canopy closes. Several successive crops could in fact be raised in this way before the trees shade them out. This method has been developed in some tropical countries under the name of agrisilviculture and has evolved out of the "Taungya" or shifting cultivation system.

A variation of this system could be tried where there is a demand for Christmas trees, with a final crop of Sitka spruce planted in a matrix of Norway spruce. "Respacing" would be carried out by success-ively removing the Norway spruce as Christmas trees

Table 12.10a

| AGE | MAIN CROP | | | | THINNINGS | | | | TOTAL |
	7cm	18cm	24cm	TOTAL VOLUME	7cm	18cm	24cm	TOTAL VOLUME	TOTAL VOLUME
20	64	—	—	64	11	—	—	11	75
25	91	—	—	91	42	—	—	42	133
30	132	1	—	133	40	2	—	42	175
35	170	13	—	183	37	5	—	42	225
40	190	44	—	234	34	8	—	42	276
45	180	95	7	282	27	14	—	42	324
50	132	156	36	324	16	19	5	40	364
55	162	190	44	396	—	—	—	—	396
60									

Table 12.10b

| AGE | MAIN CROP | | | | THINNINGS | | | | TOTAL |
	£4.75	£8.30	£11.30	TOTAL £	£4.75	£8.30	£11.30	TOTAL £ THIN-NINGS	£ per Ha.
20	304	—	—	304	52	—	—	52	356
25	432	—	—	432	200	—	—	202	632
30	627	8	—	635	190	17	—	207	842
35	808	108	—	916	176	42	—	218	1134
40	903	365	—	1268	162	66	—	228	1496
45	855	789	79	1723	128	116	11	255	1978
50	627	1294	407	2328	76	158	57	291	2619
55	770	1577	497	2844	—	—	—	—	2844
60									

Table 12.10c

| AGE | Discount Factor | MAIN CROP | | THINNINGS | | ACC. D.V. | Total Discounted Value |
		Actual Value	Discounted Value	Actual Value	Discounted Value		
20	0.377	304	115	52	20	20	135
25	0.295	432	127	200	59	79	206
30	0.231	635	147	207	48	127	274
35	0.181	916	166	218	40	167	333
40	0.142	1268	180	228	32	199	379
45	0.111	1723	191	255	28	227	418
50	0.087	2328	203	291	25	252	455
55	0.068	2844	193	—	—	252	445
60	0.054						

until only the final crop of Sitka spruce was left.
In this way a highly remunerative early return would
result from the respacing operation which would add
considerably to the overall return. Table 12.7 shows
a highly speculative suggestion of the possible out-
come of such an operation.

If the trees can be adequately protected, another
way of making use of the wasted space between final
crop trees would be to allow it to be grazed by domes-
ticated animals or even game. This alternative to
thinning is known as silvipasture and is also pract-
ised in certain parts of the world.

12.3 What type of thinning?

Whatever type of thinning is employed, it should be
at marginal intensity, which is the maximum volume that
can be removed without reducing the growing stock to a
level where volume increment cannot be maintained.
This approximates 70% of the maximum Mean Annual Increment — e.g. Yield Class.

As well as "intensity" — the average level of remov-
als — the elements in a "thinning regime" are Type and
Thinning cycle. In considering the type of thinning,
the first choice is between "selective" and "non-selective" types. In this context it is worth remembering
that a non-selective thinning is "neutral" in its
effect, that is the size-class composition remains the
same after thinning as it was before. Table 12.8 shows
the effect of a "neutral" thinning.

More control can be effected over the development of
a crop by selective thinning. In a "low" thinning a
larger number of smaller than average-sized trees are
removed to make up the same volume, resulting in a crop
of larger than average-sized trees. In a "crown" thinning, on the other hand, a smaller number of larger-
sized trees is removed. This results in a crop of
smaller-sized trees. Such a thinning may be an advantage at the beginning, when the smaller sizes are unsaleable, but later on, due to the larger number of
smaller trees in the crop, it could be a disadvantage.

Tables 12.9 and 12.10 show the effects on the development of the crop and its value of these two types of
thinning. From these it can be seen that while the
total volume production is the same, the proportion in
the different categories varies and this affects the
value. The maximum discounted revenue for the "low"
thinning is £488, the "non-selective" is £474 and the
"crown" thinning is £455. The rotation of maximum
D.R. for the "crown" and "non-selective" is 50 years
and for the "low" thinning is 55 years as the last
tends to lengthen the rotation.

Often, of course, a combination of types may be used
in practice with a "low" or "neutral" thinning in the
early stages, followed later by a "crown" thinning.
In this way, the forester has far greater control over
the development of the crop and can vary his methods
to suit changes in the market.

Chapter 13

13.1   Choice of Rotation.

The "rotation" is defined as being the number of
years between the establishment of a tree crop,
whether by planting or natural regeneration, and its
final felling. Under the old, "classical" systems of
silviculture, where the objective was a "normal" forest in which all age classes are equally represented,
a rigid, predetermined rotation was essential. As the
forest was divided up from the beginning into annual
felling areas, or "coupes", the rotation had to be
decided beforehand and strictly adhered to.

In these circumstances, obviously, no decision as to
when to fell the crop had to be made by the forester.
In those days conditions were very different. Everything was much more settled, rates of interest were
low, costs and prices fixed and a very low rate of inflation. Today, however, things are very different.

To meet these changing conditions, present day systems of forest management are more flexible and prag-
matic. While there is still an advantage to have some
idea of the rotation being aimed at, the actual age of
the final felling is less critical. In actual fact,
the culmination of the maximum Mean annual increment,

or the net discounted revenue, is on a fairly flat
curve and the reduction in value of felling five years
earlier or later does not make that much difference.
If market conditions change appreciably, a rise in
prices could offset the expected loss. To take advantage of changing conditions, much more flexibility is
needed and decision-making by the forest manager is
essential.

Generally, six types of rotation are recognised:
Physical, Technical, Silvicultural, Maximum Volume
production, Highest average income and Financial. They
are defined as:
Physical Rotation: The natural life-span of the trees.
On some sites this could be a lot shorter, for example due to the liability to windblow.

Technical: The length of time needed to grow trees to
a particular size to meet the specifications of a
certain market - pulpwood, saw timber or veneer logs.

Silvicultural: The rotation most favourable for natural regeneration. The age at which maximum viable
seed is produced is usually long before the end of
its life-span and could also be before the culmination of volume production.

Maximum Volume production: Taken literally this would
be the same as the physical rotation, but usually
what is meant is the rotation of maximum mean annual
increment.

Maximum average income: This is, in effect, the rotation of maximum volume production expressed in money
terms. Depending on the price/size gradient, it
could be shorter or longer than that expressed in
volume terms.

Financial Rotation: This is the criterion most generally used in financial calculations and is the
rotation of maximum net discounted revenue. The
length of this rotation will be very much affected by
the rate of compound discount used.

The decision at the time of planting as to the length of the rotation to be aimed at, will depend on the objects of management. The purpose for which the crop is being grown will determine the type of rotation to be used.

13.2 When to fell a mature crop.

Although the general decision as to the length of rotation will have been made earlier in the life of a crop - perhaps even before planting - the final decision may be made nearer to the time of the actual felling. The state of the market and other considerations can be taken into account to give a flexible approach.

The realistic way to decide whether a crop should be felled is to find out whether there would be a higher net return then or by leaving it until later. It should be remembered that any future expected returns would have to be discounted to allow for the "cost of waiting". Examples are shown, using figures from the Money Yield Table (Table 5.4) for Sitka spruce (Y.C. 12).

(a) At age 45
     Present value of crop   £2,314 per hectare
     Value of thinnings carried
     out now   £ 249
     Value of crop if felled in
     5 years time £2903 x 0.783 =   £2,273
     (Actual value discounted
      for 5 years)
     Total of thinnings plus
     felling in 5 years time   £2,522 per hectare
     Return is greater in 5 years,
     so do not fell.

(b) At age 50
     Present value of crop   £2,903 per hectare
     Value of thinnings   £ 273
     Value of crop if felled in
     5 years time £3428 x 0.783 =   £2,684
     Total of thinnings plus

felling in 5 years time   £2,957 per hectare
Marginally better - £54 - <u>so</u>
<u>discretion should be used</u>
whether to fell or not.

(c) <u>At age 55</u>
Present value of crop   £3,428 per hectare
Value of thinnings   £ 261
Value of crop if felled in
5 years time £3876 x 0.783 = £3,034
Total of thinnings plus
felling in 5 years time   £3,295 per hectare
Decidedly less value in 5
years time so <u>should def-</u>
<u>initely be felled now.</u>

Another way of deciding whether to fell, is to use the
Indicating Percent. If the value of the increment, expressed as a percentage of the average growing stock
falls below the Internal Rate of Return for the crop,
it should be felled.

Indicating percent = <u>Average annual value of the</u>
<u>increment</u> x 100
Average value of the growing
stock

By using the post-thinning value of the first measurement and the pre-thinning value for the second measurement, the indicating percent at the three ages calculated above are:

(d) <u>Age 45</u> $\dfrac{£2903 - 2065 \div 5}{£2903 + 2065 \div 2}$ x 100 = $\dfrac{167.6}{2484}$ x 100

$= \underline{6.75\%}$

(e) <u>Age 50</u> $\dfrac{£3428 - 2630 \div 5}{£3428 + 2630 \div 2}$ x 100 = $\dfrac{159.6}{3029}$ x 100

$= \underline{5.27\%}$

(f) <u>Age 55</u> $\dfrac{£3876 - 3167 \div 5}{£3876 + 3167 \div 2}$ x 100 = $\dfrac{141.8}{3521.5}$ x 100

$= \underline{4.27\%}$

If the IRR of the crop is calculated to be 5.2%, then
it is marginally above at age 50 but definitely below
at age 55.

13.3 When to replace an uneconomic crop.

The general principles of how to make this decision
have been shown in an earlier chapter (9.2) and are
summarised as - "Fell when the sum of the Discounted
Revenue of the existing crop and the Net discounted
revenue of the replacement crop, reaches a maximum."

If a crop of Scots pine (Yield Class 6) is growing
on a site that could produce Sitka spruce (Y.C.12),
when should it be felled and replaced? The answer will
depend very much on the point in the rotation at which
it is being considered. Two sets of calculations are
shown in Tables 13.1 and 13.2 considering the position
at age 20 and age 40 respectively.

From these figures it can be seen that at age 20, it
would be best to fell and replace at age 30. At age
40, however, it would be worth delaying it further
until age 55.

In both these cases, the 'realisation' value of the
existing crop has been used and discounted back over
the appropriate number of years rather than using the
Discounted Revenue figure taken from the start of the
rotation. This considers the position as it is at
that age, rather than looking back to the start.

Table 13.3 shows the position where the crop of
Scots pine (Y.C.6) is to be replaced by Douglas fir
(Y.C.14). In this case replacement should take place
immediately at either age, for in fact there would be
a definite reduction in revenue by waiting further.
So, generally, one can say that the more valuable the
replacement crop the sooner it should be effected.

Table 13.1

Age	Realis- ation value	Years to be dis- counted	Dis- count factor	Discoun- ted Real- isation value	NDR Suc- cessor crop	Total	
20	185	0	1.000	185	83	268	
25	337	5	0.783	264	65	329	
30	508	10	0.614	312	51	363	Optimum age
35	633	15	0.481	305	40	345	
40	808	20	0.377	305	31	336	
45	1063	25	0.295	319	26	345	
50	1422	30	0.231	328	19	347	
55	1818	35	0.181	329	15	344	
60	2239	40	0.142	318	12	330	
65	2642	45	0.111	293	9	302	

Table 13.2

Age	Realis- ation value	Years to be dis- counted	Dis- count factor	Discoun- ted Real- isation value	NDR Suc- cessor crop	Total	
40	808	0	1.000	808	83	891	
45	1063	5	0.783	832	65	897	
50	1422	10	0.614	873	51	924	
55	1818	15	0.487	885	40	925	Optimum age
60	2239	20	0.377	844	31	875	
65	2642	25	0.295	779	26	805	

Table 13.3a

At age 20

Age	Dis- counted Realis- ation value	NDR suc- cessor crop	Total	
20	185	413	598	Optimum
25	264	334	598	
30	312	254	566	
35	305	199	504	
40	305	156	461	
45	319	122	441	
50	328	96	424	
55	329	75	404	
60	318	59	377	
65	293	46	338	

Table 13.3b

At age 40

Age	Dis- counted Realis- ation value	NDR suc- cessor crop	Total	
40	808	413	1221	Optimum
45	832	334	1166	
50	873	254	1127	
55	885	199	1084	
60	844	122	1000	
65	779	122	901	

13.4   Conversion of a forest to agriculture or other non-forestry use.

The same general principle would apply if a forest crop is to be converted to some other use. If the profitability of the new use is sufficiently high an immediate change would be an advantage. Otherwise, it may well pay better to delay the felling until the original crop is nearer its culmination.

Chapter 14

14.1   Brashing

Brashing consists of the removal of the dead lower
branches of trees, usually conifers, after the canopy
has closed and before the first thinning. Although it
is a form of pruning, its main purpose is not to produce knot-free timber, but to give easy access into
the wood. If brashing is carried out before the first
thinnings are marked, the persons doing the marking
and measuring have a much easier task as anyone who
has tried to push through an unbrashed Sitka spruce
plantation will know.

If brashing is combined with marking the first thinning, only those trees to be left in are brashed. In
this way, after the thinning has been done a high proportion of the crop will be brashed.

The need for brashing is confined to selective thinnings, as in non-selective methods - such as 'line'
thinning - no marking is done and the trees are felled
into the space already cleared.

Brashing is usually done to a height of about 1.8m,
or to the nearest whorl below that height. This gives
sufficient "head-room" for passage through the crop.

Brashing to this height, of 70 to 90% of the trees,
costs something in the order of £35 to £90 per hectare,
depending on the species. Larch is easily done and
can even be done by knocking with a stout stick. Sitka
spruce, on the other hand, has to be done with a saw.
The extremes are thus Larch at 2 - 3p per tree and
Sitka spruce 3 - 4p.

If the average volume per tree removed in a first
thinning is about $0.08m^3$, the cost per m^3 works out at
something between 38p and 50p. However, this may well
be set-off against the reduction in the cost of marking
and measuring. If the cost of marking and measuring is
reduced by up to 50p per m^3, then it is obviously worth
doing.

Another factor to be considered is that of "window-
dressing". It is possible that where the thinnings
are to be sold standing, no merchant will be prepared
to make an offer for an unbrashed wood or only at a
much reduced price. This would not apply, of course,
if a non-selective thinning is to be done.

On many private estates where 100% brashing is carried-out, this is not for silvicultural reasons but
for game-management. It means that the beaters have
easy access. In this case, it would be fairer if at
least part of the cost of brashing were changed against
the sporting rents rather than forestry operations.

Brashing can also be done for fire-protection purposes, particularly in fire-breaks, to prevent ground
fires from spreading into the crowns. Here, obviously,
it should be a charge against fire protection. Brashing can also be done for amenity purposes, particularly
alongside "scenic drives" where the roadside trees are
brashed - and even high-pruned - to give a better vis-
ual impression than an impenetrable barrier of branches.

In financial terms, therefore, the decision as to
whether to brash or not is simply a matter of weighing
the costs against the benefits. If it is too costly,
then an alternative such as non-selective thinning may
have to be used. This can always be followed by a sel-

ective thinnings in later stages.

14.2 High-pruning.

Unlike brashing, this is carried out for the prime
purpose of producing high-quality knot-free timber.
It is usually confined to the final crop trees and up
to a pruning height of 7m can be done in three "lifts".
The first "lift" being at about 20 years (2 to 4m), the
second at about 25 years (4 to 6m) and the third at
about 30 years (6 to 7m).

Since high-pruning is only worth doing if sufficient
"premium" is paid for knot-free timber, it is essential
to know exactly how the cost compares with the increased price. To do this, costs of pruning must be compounded to the end of the rotation, related to the
final crop volume and the price paid. To illustrate
this, a number of worked examples are set out below:

(a) Corsican pine (Y.C.14)
     Rotation 50 years. Final crop 396 stems per
     hectare and volume of 400m^3. Pruning in three
     lifts, at 15 years (@ 4p per stem), 20 years (5p)
     and 25 years (3p). What premium over the normal
     sale price is needed to justify this action?

     The costs for pruning at each "lift" are com-
     pounded to the end of the rotation, totalled and
     divided by the final volume to give the cost per
     m^3. If the "premium" is more than this amount,
     then it is worth carrying out the pruning.

Table 14.1

Age of lift	Years to end of Rotation	Stems per Hectare	Cost of Pruning per Stem	Cost per Hectare	Compound Factor	Compounded Costs
15	35	396	4p	£15.84	5.516	£87.37
20	30	396	5p	£19.80	4.320	£85.54
25	25	396	3p	£11.88	3.386	£40.23
						£ 213.14

Volume per hectare: 400m^3. Cost per hectare
£213.14.
Cost per m^3 = £213.14 ÷ 400 = £0.53 or 53p.
So, in this case the premium would have to be
more than 53p per m^3.

(b) Scots pine (Y.C.6)
Rotation 80 years. Final crop 570 stems per
hectare and volume of 265m^3. Pruning in three
lifts, as before, at the same costs. What
premium would be needed in this case?

Table 14.2

Age of lift	Years to end of Rotation	Stems per Hectare	Cost of Pruning per Stem	Cost per Hectare	Compound Factor	Compounded Costs
15	65	570	4p	£22.80	23.840	£543.55
20	60	570	5p	£28.50	18.679	£532.35
25	55	570	3p	£17.10	14.635	£250.26
						£ 1326.16

Volume per hectare 265m^3. Cost per hectare
£1326.16.
Cost per m^3 = £1326 ÷ 265 = £5.00. So, in
this case the premium would have to be at least
£5 per m^3.

While in the first case it might well be possible
to get an extra 50p per m^3, it is highly unlikely
that in the second case an extra £5 per m^3 would
be paid by a merchant. In these circumstances,
high pruning Scots pine of that yield class would
be a complete waste of money.

(c) Poplar (Y.C.14)
This quick-growing broadleaved crop has been
grown for many years in Britain specially for the
match-making industry. However, recently this
market has "dried-up" and alternative uses are
being sought. It appears that sawlogs of poplar

are quite suitable for internal joinery work and this may be a future for this crop. Being fast growing, it is usually planted at final spacing (17.3m) and grown without thinning. Due to the wide spacing, high-pruning is essential, if reasonably knot-free timber is to be produced. A calculation on the cost of such pruning shows as follows:

Rotation 35 years. Final crop 185 stems per hectare and volume 460m³. If pruning is carried out at ages 5, 10 and 15 years at the same costs as before, what is the cost per m³?

Table 14.3

Age	No. of years to end of Rotation	No. of stems per Hectare	Cost of Pruning per Stem	Cost per Hectare	Compound Factor	Compounded cost per Hectare
5	30	185	4p	£7.40	4.320	£31.96
10	25	185	5p	£9.25	3.386	£31.32
15	20	185	9p	£5.55	2.653	£14.72
			Total cost per hectare		=	£ 78.00

$$\text{Cost per m}^3 = \frac{78}{4600} = 17p$$

So, owing to the high-yield, reduced number of stems to be pruned and short rotation, it is obviously worthwhile pruning such a crop. It is likely to have an NDR (@ 5%) of £577 per hectare and an IRR of 7%.

Chapter 15

15.1   The Costs and Benefits of Forest Roads.

One of the heaviest items of capital expenditure in
the forest is the construction of roads. These can
vary from £1,500 per kilometre for "low specification"
roads, not much better than tracks suitable for four-
wheel drive vehicles in dry conditions, to £6,000 per
kilometre for "high specification" roads suitable for
articulated lorries with a load of 32 tonnes in all
weathers.

While the actual siting and construction of roads is
an engineering problem, the density of roads and their
position in relation to the crop is a decision to be
made by the forest manager. The cost of road construction will largely depend on the terrain and the specification to be used, but its financial justification
will depend on the volume and value of the crop. Obviously, the more valuable the crop, the greater the
justification for spending money on road construction.

The "density" of roading is usually expressed as so
many kilometres of road per square kilometre of forest
(km/km^2). The average spacing between roads is the
reciprocal of the density, that is if the density is
$x km/km^2$ then the average spacing is $1/x$ km. On flat

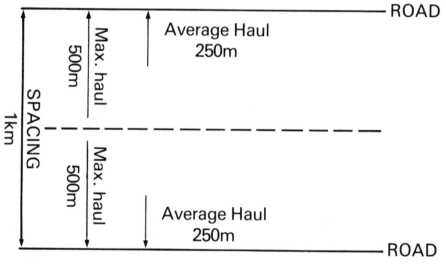

Figure 15.1

ground, the <u>maximum</u> haul would be half the spacing,
and the <u>average</u> haul a quarter of the spacing. If the
density were $1km/km^2$, the spacing would be 1,000m, the
maximum haul 500m and the average haul 250m. This is
illustrated in <u>Figure 15.1</u>. On steep ground, however,
where haulage is only possible in one direction, these
figures would be double.

The relationship between density, spacing, maximum
and average length of haul is shown in <u>Table 15.2</u>.
Assuming a figure of £6,000 per kilometre for road
construction and £2 per m^3 per 100m haul, columns 4 and
5 show the relevant costs for a range of densities.

From these figures it can be seen that the higher
the density of roading the higher the overall cost of
road construction per unit area. At the same time,
the higher the density of roading the lower the cost
of hauling timber from stump to the roadside. The
optimum density of roading is thus a balance between
the two and the graph (<u>Figure 15.3</u>) shows this relationship. The most economical density of roading is
where the sum of costs for roads and movement is at a
minimum. In the next section, a number of examples
have been worked out to show the effects of differing
circumstances.

15.2   <u>Optimum Road Density</u>.

The variables in determining the optimum roading
density are:

(a)   Cost of road construction
(b)   Cost of haulage to the road and
(c)   Volume production per hectare.

The examples shown in <u>Table 15.2</u> and <u>Figure 15.3</u>
assumed a cost of road-construction of £6,000 per km,
a haulage cost of £2 per m^3 per 100m and an annual
volume out-turn of $10m^3$ per hectare. In the following
examples these assumptions have been varied to see the
effect on the optimum roading density.

<u>Example 1</u>. What would be the effect if the annual vol-
ume out-turn was doubled?

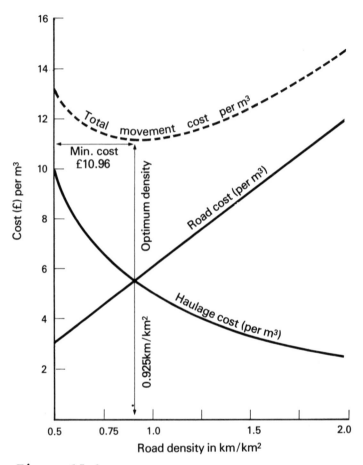

Figure 15.3

By doubling the volume out-turn, the road costs per m^3 are halved. The extraction costs to roadside remain the same so the combined movement cost is lower and the optimum density is increased to 1.5km per km^2.

Table 15.1   (Example 1)

Road Density	Road Costs per ha.	Road Costs per m^3 (£)	Haulage Costs per m^3	Total Movement Costs	
0.5	30	1.50	10.00	11.50	
1.0	60	3.00	5.00	8.00	
1.5	90	4.50	3.30	7.80	*
2.0	120	6.00	2.50	8.50	
2.5	150	7.50	2.00	9.50	

* Minimum

Example 2.   What would be the position if road construction costs were £10,000 per km and extraction costs were £3 per m^3 per 100m? Annual volume out-turn remaining at $10m^3$ per ha.

Table 15.2   Optimum Road Density   (Example 2)

Road Density (km/km^2)	Spacing (m)	Max. distance Haul (m)	Av. distance Haul (m)	Road Cost per hectare (£)	Road Cost per m^3 (£)	Haulage Cost per (m^3) (£)	Total movement cost per m^3 (£)
0.5	2000	1000	500	30	3.00	10.00	13.00
0.75	1333	666	333	45	4.50	6.60	11.10
1.0	1000	500	250	60	6.00	5.00	11.00*
1.5	660	330	165	90	9.00	3.30	12.30
2.0	500	250	125	120	12.00	2.50	14.50
2.5	400	200	100	150	15.00	2.00	17.00

*Minimum

Assumptions:

   Cost of road construction: £6,000 per km

   Haulage costs: £2 per m³ per 100m

   Annual Volume production: 10m³ per hectare.

   *From Figure 15.3 it can be seen that in fact the
   minimum is £10.96 per m³ at a density of 0.925km/
   km², but the variation between 0.75 and 1.0 is
   very slight.

Since road construction costs and haulage costs
have both risen by approximately the same proportion,
while the combined movement cost per m³ has risen, the
optimum density remains the same at about 1km per km².

Table 15.5

Road Density (km/km²)	Spacing (m)	Av. Haul (m)	Road Costs per ha. (£)	Road Costs per m³ (£)	Haulage Costs per m³ (£)	Total Costs per m³ (£)	
0.5	2000	500	50	5.00	15.00	20.00	} M
0.75	1333	333	75	7.50	10.00	17.50	} i n
1.0	1000	250	100	10.00	7.50	17.50	i
1.25	800	200	125	12.50	6.00	18.50	m u m

Example 3. If road construction costs remain at
£6,000 per km and volume out-turn at 10m³ per hectare
per annum, but extraction costs are doubled to £4 per
m³ per 100m, what is the optimum density now?

   As the cost of extraction increases, so a higher
density of roading becomes justified. In this particular case a density of 1.25 km per km² is the
optimum.

Table 15.6   (Example 3)

Road Density	Spacing	Av. Haul	Road Costs per ha.	Road Costs per m^3	Haulage Costs m^3	Total Costs m^3	
0.5	2000	500	30	3.00	20.00	23.00	M
1.0	1000	250	60	6.00	10.00	16.00	i
1.25	800	200	75	7.50	8.00	15.50	n i
1.5	660	165	90	9.00	6.60	15.60	m u
1.75	570	143	105	10.50	5.70	16.22	m
2.0	500	125	120	12.00	5.00	17.00	

This particular example, where extraction costs are double, would be similar to a case where on a slope only one way extraction is possible. In that case, the maximum haul becomes the average haul and costs will increase accordingly.

It should be appreciated that all these examples have been calculated from basic principles, by perhaps crude and unsophisticated methods. More refined formulae have been evolved by the Forestry Commission, but the same principles are used.

15.3   When to put in roads.

Roads, like the land itself, are part of the capital asset which may be available for several rotations of crop. Therefore, it can be argued that the cost of putting them in should not be charged wholly against a single rotation. In this case, the timing of construction is not so critical from the point of view of compound interest/discount. This is the "whole forest" point of view where the objective is to build up a "normal" forest which would go on in perpetuity.

However, more often it may be thought of as a single rotation plantation, where costs are all chargeable against a single set of receipts. In which case, of

course, timing can make a vital difference to the
net discounted revenue. The later in the rotation the
costs occur, the more they are discounted in the financial calculations.

From this point of view, road construction is usually carried-out in time for the first commercial
thinning, probably about two years beforehand. If the
first thinning is to be done in year 20, then road
construction costs will be discounted 18 years in NDR
calculations. The discount factor for 18 years at 5%
is 0.415, which means that less than half the actual
costs are used in the calculation. This could make a
large difference to the NDR, a difference between
profit and loss.

The usual practice has been for the road layout to
be planned at an early stage, before planting is carried out, so that the proposed road-lines may be left
unplanted. Then the actual construction can be done
before thinning takes place. Another advantage in
delaying actual construction has been the rapid development in extraction techniques. Layouts planned
originally for horse extraction, may in fact be found
suitable for cable-crane use by the time the roads are
actually built. This could mean that the number of
roads needed is far less than at first considered necessary.

It is also possible that changes in the market for
small round-wood could occur during the period which
might make thinnings uneconomic and road construction
could be delayed still further until just before the
final felling.

While the prime purpose for roads in the forest is
for removing the timber, they can also be used for
other purposes such as access and fire-fighting. In
some cases it may be advisable to put in low specification roads even before planting to give access to
the site. These roads could then be strengthened for
lorry traffic before the time of first thinning. This
would be one way of meeting the need at minimum overall cost.

In the case of private estates where forestry and
agriculture are integrated, many of the roads may be
used for both purposes and costs can be shared between
them. In some cases, also, where such a road may be
of public benefit, at least part of the road may in
fact be taken over by the local authority.

15.4 Maintenance of roads.

While there can be some argument as to the charging
of the capital cost of road construction to a single
rotation, the cost of annual maintenance is obviously
chargeable to the rotation.

The amount of maintenance work needed on the roads
will depend on the amount of use they have and the
weight of traffic. Obviously some roads will only
need repairs once in five years - immediately after a
thinning - while other, "feeder", roads may need work
every year. For financial calculations, as in determining the NDR of a crop, the annual maintenance cost
is more easily used as a capitalised sum which can be
added to the construction cost. Such a sum is, in
effect, the capital that would have to be invested to
produce the annual return.

Most forest roads are of earth or gravel surfaces
which can be easily maintained by scraping with a
"grader". This reshapes the bearing-surface and
cleans-out the ditches mechanically. A certain amount
of other work on ditches and culverts would also have
to be done from time-to-time, particularly after heavy
rain storms. Even so the average annual maintenance
cost would be somewhere in the order of £40 to £50 per
kilometre. At a density of $1km/km^2$ this would work
out at 40p to 50p per hectare per annum. Such an
annual figure, if capitalised, would represent a sum
of £8 to £10 to be added to the construction cost.

If, instead of thinking of the roads as a single
rotation investment, a "whole forest" approach is made
then all road costs could be thought of as normal capital. In this case, an annual "write-off" figure
could be calculated on the basis of the actual life of

the road. If it were thought that such a road would
last for, say, 50 years before major reconstruction,
then the total capital sum could be divided by this
figure to give an annual cost. In such a forest, of
course, that went on in perpetuity, only simple interest would be chargeable rather than compound interest.
In which case an annual charge would be more suitable
than a capital sum.

Chapter 16

16.1   The forest manager's task.

A manager's main task is to achieve the "objects of management" laid down by the owner of the enterprise, whether it is an individual, a company, or the state. If he is successful, few questions will be asked, but if he fails he will have to justify his actions and if he cannot do so, will in all probability lose his job.

The prime objective in forestry is to grow trees to produce timber, whatever the secondary objectives may be. The forest manager thus has to try to produce as much timber as possible, as quickly and economically as possible, within the various constraints imposed. To do this he has to make decisions, and to be successful he must make the right decisions. In forestry, making the right decisions is even more important than in most other enterprises, because of the long time-scale involved. The manager may not even live long enough to see the full implications of his decisions.

While some people are able to make the right decisions, almost by instinct, most people need some sort of help. The financial "tools", described in this book, give the manager some sort of objective backing

in making these decisions. So if he fails, he can at
least show that the decision was the right one in those
circumstances.

Nevertheless, the decision is his and his alone and
he stands or falls by the decision. There is no substitute for experience and human judgement, but some
sort of objective "yardstick" does give the manager
some guidance and backing. He must not blame his tools
if things go wrong, remembering that only a bad workman
does that.

When electronic computers were first introduced, they
tended to be regarded with awe as some sort of super-
human "brain". However, people who have received com-
puterised electricity bills for £2,000, when it should
have been £20, know only too well that they are capable
of making mistakes! Computers can do simple arithmetic
incredibly quickly, but the proper interpretation and
application of the data depends on human judgement. If
rubbish is fed in, rubbish will come out. Exactly the
same applies to the use of the "tools" described in
this book.

16.2   The financial "tools".

Making decisions involves only the present and the
future, for past decisions cannot be changed. Decisions involving the future are particularly difficult,
as it does not yet exist. However carefully and pain-
stakingly a forecast is made, there is no guarantee
that things will work out as expected. The further
one peers into the future, the more nebulous it becomes. This is the main problem in forestry where the
length of time involved is much longer than in most
other forms of enterprise.

Consequently, most of the "tools" used are to do with
the passage of time and its effect on the present value
of future expectations. Since compound interest/dis-
count does reflect the effects of time, it is used in
such calculations. So long as the limitations of using
it are known, it can be a guide in coming to the right
decisions.

The two basic "tools" described have been "Net discounted revenue" and the "Internal rate of return".
Each has its place in decision-making and worked examples have been given to show where they are appropriate.
Both are dependant on the "Price/size gradient" and the
"Volume yield tables". The latter have been worked out
empirically from measurements of actual plantations and
can be used with reasonable certainty to forecast rates
of growth, provided that conditions are similar. The
former, however, depends entirely on the "state of the
market" which can be much more erratic. Long term
trends can be forecast more easily than variations from
year to year. Even so, certain markets on which much
reliance has been placed in the past, can disappear almost overnight and be replaced by others completely
unforeseen.

Other "tools" described include the return on capital
invested - measured in various ways - and the Indicating percent. Again, examples have been shown of ways
in which these can be used to help in decision-making.

16.3   Making decisions.

In any form of management, decision-making is largely
a matter of comparing cost and benefit. Where the benefit outweighs the cost, then it is worth doing. If
the extra cost of a particular course of action is more
than the resulting benefit, then it is not worth doing.
Basically, it is as simple as that.   Money is a useful
"yardstick", easily understood by all.

However, there are some benefits which are not so
easily put into money terms. These are the environ-
mental, aesthetic and recreational benefits, which
affect not only the owners of the enterprise but also
the public at large.

One way of measuring the value of such benefits is
to calculate the "opportunity cost" of foregoing certain revenues in order to meet the requirements of
these benefits. For example, if it is environmentally
and aesthetically desirable to grow a less commercially
valuable crop - such as broadleaved trees - where a

highly productive crop of Sitka spruce could be grown, then the "opportunity cost" is the difference between the NDR in the two cases. This can then be set against the benefit resulting from the action.

Using the "tools" cannot guarantee results and in the end it is the experience and judgement of the forest manager that counts. No one can accurately foresee the future, but at least by using some system of logical thought, some of the uncertainty can be taken out of the guesswork.

HART, C. E.,   "British Timber Prices and
                 Forestry Costings"

                                 Coleford 1979

HAMILTON, G.J. and
CHRISTIE, J.M., "Forest Management Tables (Metric)"

                                 H.M.S.O. 1971

-"-   "Influence of Spacing on Crop
                 Characteristics and Yield"

                                 H.M.S.O. 1974

MOORE, D.G.,   "The Oceanic Forest: A Study
                 in Profitability"

                                 Scottish Forestry
                                 Vol. 27 No.2,
                                 April 1973